# Just Words
## The Us and Them Thing

Val Dumond

Author of *Grammar For Grownups*
and *Elements of Nonsexist Usage*

*For Dave
Harmony - one word
at a time!
Val Dumond
2006*

Muddy Puddle Press

Just Words — The Us and Them Thing
Copyright © 2005 Val Dumond
All rights reserved including the right of reproduction
in whole or in part in any form.

Some portions published as *SHEIT*
Copyright 1984
Dumond Publications

Some portions published as *Elements of Nonsexist Usage*
Copyright 1990
Prentice Hall and colophons are registered trademarks of
Simon & Schuster, Inc.


First Edition
Printed in the United States


ISBN 0-9679704-4-X

Muddy Puddle Press
P O Box 97124
Tacoma WA 98497

Library of Congress Cataloging-in-Publication Data:
Available from publisher.

Dumond, Val
    *Just Words — The Us and Them Thing*
    A guide to inclusive spoken and written
    English/Val Dumond
    Includes Index and Glossary
    ISBN 0-9679704-4-X
    1. English language — Usage. 2. Nonsexist language.
    3. Nonracist language. 4. Nonageist language.
    5. Nondiscriminating language. 6. Inclusive language.

# Contents

# Other Books by Val Dumond

*Grammar For Grownups*

*Elements of Nonsexist Usage*

*SHEIT*

*Doin' The Puyallup*

*Steilacoom's Church*

*Olympia Coloring Book*

*Mush On and Smile (a novel)*

*How We Fought World War II at
William T. Sherman Elementary School*

# Introduction

Words! Words! Words!

What if words and their impact could lead to world peace, family harmony and social justice? *Yeah sure!* you say.

*Why not?* I answer. It could happen. What it takes is an awareness of the Us and Them Thing and, with it, the recognition of the importance of chosing courteous and respectful words.

That's what this book is about — understanding the Us and Them Thing in order to come one step closer to those lofty goals. World peace — one word at a time!

Using language to discuss language is tricky. We may not agree on which language to use. And while we may agree on "English," are we really speaking "English" or are we using a modified version? (Early Americans blanched at the thought of using "the king's language.")

While we in the United States basically use the English language, we have made it our own, a kind of American English. Add to that words borrowed from every country in the world, the shades of meaning in certain words, and the multiple meanings of other words, and you begin to get a sense of the problem of communicating with words.

vi / *Just Words*

*What did you intend to say?*
*My understanding is ...*
*I'm not sure what you mean by that.*
*What does that word mean?*
*I always thought that word was offensive.*

We use words to express ourselves, our feelings, our anxieties, our hopes, our views. We use words to explain, complain, plead, lie, cover up, share, expose, inquire, support, tear apart, hurt, heal, apologize, blame, praise, compliment, destroy, build, acknowledge, sell, flatter...

[Whenever I find a list of words such as the above, I go over them slowly, as the author did when dreaming them up. That provides a clearer sense of the purpose behind all those words. And after all, they are "just words."]

Confusion about what words are acceptable (let's get rid of "politically correct") continues to grow as Americans grapple with problems of diversity. Often regarded as "our differences," we stretch to accommodate them. But is that necessary? Or even helpful? This book offers a way to adopt inclusive language to eliminate or at least reduce the bias in communication of gender, race, nationality, class, age and religion.

*Just Words* emphasizes the need to accept the ways we are different, focus on the ways we are alike, and concentrate on ways to respect individuality — all through words. *Just Words* offers suggestions to express ourselves to stay within the law and to avoid hurting others. This book deals as much with attitude behind words as it does with the words themselves. The trick is to accept diversity rather than disengage from it.

*Just Words* is about the Us and Them Thing, based on the natural inclination of people to embrace *Us* and be wary of *Them*.

The word "Americans" is used in this book to mean people in the United States, while recognizing that all people living in the Western Hemisphere are all considered Americans (Canadians, Mexicans, Venezuelans, Brazilians, Panamanians, Peruvians, etc.).

In the U.S., a nation founded by social outcasts and built by immigrants from around the world, people are challenged to treasure simultaneously their own heritage and the differences of others. This ideal nation — the only nation of the world entirely comprised of people from some place else — places high value on the ways each of us lays claim to our own uniqueness.

At the same time, ideally, we need to cherish the differences, honor and respect all people. The author intends this book to apply to the Americans who live in the U.S., those we consider to be *Us* — all of us.

However, humans being human beings, people sometimes fear differences, are afraid to recognize someone who isn't just like *Us*. These fears often result in outbursts of language (and worse). What often appears as opposition may in fact be a defense. The shorthand word we use to discuss those people who are not like Us is *Them*.

That briefly is how Americans regard themselves. Some are *Us* and some are *Them*. We feel safer that way.

This book looks into the ways that bias has been built into our language over the years — in gender, race, age, class, people with disabilities, and people from other countries. (You'll find, ironically, that we all come from other countries.)

Consider the power of language and the preferred power of inclusive language. In the very first chapter you'll find some guidelines on ways to look at word usage to show how some words can be as dangerous as swords and other words can be as healing as medication. In the second chapter, you'll find a review of the powerful ways that words lead to images which then form attitudes and are the links to behavior.

Chapter 3 shows how words can become a habit. We become used to voicing certain words, only to discover that they no longer are appropriate. We use words that have gone "out of style," words whose meanings have changed into something else. Slang is not a part of this work because it changes with time and location. "Cool" may mean one thing in New York and something else in Los Angeles, one thing to a 50-year-old and quite another to a teenager. A speaker may think they're using one word with a particular meaning and the listener may interpret that word with an entirely different meaning.

In the same way, words gain and lose power with usage, even becoming dangerous when they exclude. (*We* are *Us*, the insiders, the accepted. *They* are *Them*, the outsiders, the unacceptable.)

Even words meant to be kind can exclude. *Adults Only* can say, "This is an orderly neighborhood; we don't want kids coming in and messing it up." *Mankind* loudly affirms that this is a male civilization where women are tolerated. *Family Entertainment* can mean "Gays and lesbians stay away." *American Pie* implies it's not to be eaten by "outsiders." The joke is that we're all outsiders, with the possible exception of the American Indian. "Possible" implies that even American Indians came from someplace else.

Some call biased language *ism-talk*, the language of sexism, racism, nationalism, classism or ageism. Others call it *exclusive*, referring to the words that exclude the other. Several words were considered for a title for this book: *Correct, Respectful, Us and Them, The Ism-words, Prejudice, Bias-free, Impartial, Fair*, and the ever-popular *Politically Correct*. All of these words are used generously in any discussion about language in America. However, the title *Just Words* was chosen not only because of the social implication of justice and fairness, but because the use of certain words in certain situations is covered by law. Unfortunately, this culture has come to the sad state of having to legislate the use of words — where and when they are used and how they are used. Do these regulations really work? Do they help break down barriers of disrespect or do they tend to strengthen them?

There are alternatives to regulations, as there are alternatives to using unjust, unkind, ungenerous words. One way: Take those last three negative adjectives (unjust, unkind, ungenerous) and change them to the positive: *fair, respectful* and *magnanimous.* Can the solution be as simple as that?

This book isn't meant to offer right and wrong talk. This is an exercise in awareness — becoming aware of the impact of words, the repercussions that result from the language we use every day.

Using alternatives requires paying attention to positive, supportive words. To focus on the positive requires patience, because time is needed to turn around the thought process of a nation, to reverse infectious hatred and turn it into tolerance and open-mindedness. That's a good word — *open-mindedness.* It connotes leaving room for new ideas, wider thought, greater understanding and, finally, acceptance of others as they are.

*Open-mindedness* implies that both young and old understand that each has walked or will walk the same path in time, that women and men stand side by side, that skin color is a matter of melanin, that sexual orientation is inborn, and that thought processes and their resulting beliefs are personal areas which must be protected.

Ever the optimists are those who believe that humans possess the brain capacity to make room in the world for people who are not like themselves. Could you imagine a world of clones, all resembling one individual? And if you could, who would that individual be — you? How would you like to live in a world populated completely by you?

Okay, that's a chilling thought for anyone. Let's get down to work and look at this business of words. In particular, we'll focus on the Us and Them Thing.

The language of stereotyping is the topic of Chapter 4. Putting people into neat boxes with labels results in a form of verbal abuse. While making language easier and quicker, stereotypical words more often are confining words that leave little wiggle room for variety. *Blue-eyed blonds* are beautiful. *Bald-headed youth* are destructive. *Old* people are tiddely. *Quakers* are submissive. *Latinos* are hot lovers. *Indians* are lazy. *Turtles* are slow. Stereo-typical words are addressed from many angles, with a discussion about how to categorize and sort the isms.

In Chapter 5, we talk about the outright hate words, the damaging, beastly, obscene words, and how they are as hurtful to the speaker as they are to the target. The language of hate is perhaps the ugliest part of America, a language of envy, pride, suspicion, superiority and fear. These are the words that fall into the category of name-calling. Hurtful words — spewed through unseen hateful mouths, scrawled on walls, whispered into telephones — take a monstrous toll. The basest, lowest, most hideous words used by faceless hate-filled wretches demean not only themselves, but all of humankind.

Then in Chapter 6 we discuss the abusive words, those that do their dirty work through repetition, innuendo, and diminution. Subtle teasing, abusive words can be as dam-aging as outright violent ones. Words that are spread subversively by innuendo and repetition tend to under-mine and demean and lead to further abuse.

When *brainwashing* was the topic of the day, the power of words to sway, overwhelm, overpower, and convince others became evident. (That was about the same time advertising executives began to look closely at and adopt a similar process.) We discovered we can do away with swearing and name calling and still demean through the powerful repeated suggestions of weakness, sickness, inability, stupidity and incompetence. Words that demean result in lower self-esteem and are both danger-ous and damning.

[While the insidious nature of *mind control* is a com-pelling subject, we'll leave that for another day. Be as-sured that language, repetition, and degradation are the elements of choice. If some alien power wishes to divide people through mind control, the first step is to turn to the Us and Them Thing, beginning with language.]

The benign words of exclusion come in for a closer look in Chapter 7 about the way business is affected by words. How many times a day do you hear a *casual* phrase or word that offends you? How many times do you use words that may be offensive to someone else, words that are an everyday part of your business vocabulary? How often do you feel left out of advertising which targets other groups? How much business are you losing by excluding some of your potential customers?

Some words are just plain illegal. Others must be used with care. In Chapter 8 we look at the legalities of words, how to avoid *getting into trouble* with grammar police.

Finally, so that readers won't be left hanging, you will find some constructive help in Chapter 9. Here you'll find ways to find alternative language, better choices and how to make them, along with suggestions to improve your communication skills.

As a bonus, you'll find at the back of the book an Appendix, followed by a comprehensive Glossary of Terms which contains additional fuel to help you build a vocabulary of inclusive language — just words!

## The Glossary

The terms in the glossary at the back of this book are alternatives, not necessarily preferred. To know how to refer to people, ask them. Ask those of another cultural background how they prefer to be named or referred to. Believe it or not, some folks object to *Baby Boomer, elder, Gen-X, Gen-Y, senior citizen, teenybopper, juvenile.* (Some teenagers absolutely hate "teenager.") If you're uncomfortable talking with someone who is not like you, ask *them* how they wish to be called.

Not the typical self-help book, *Just Words* comes replete with suggestions for recognizing the differences between people while appreciating those same differences. Rather than a list of "Ten Ways to…" this book offers a thorough examination of the role language plays in daily discourse with people, all of whom are not Us.

Hatred and suspicion not only consume precious time but they sap strength. For proof, compare the wrinkles worn by a distrustful angry old crock and those of a considerate, cheerful, agreeable opposite who accepts folks for who they are.

Use this book as a writing tool, a reference to ensure that your written and spoken ideas are free of biased implication. Use it as a general language tool by reading it through. You'll find help in acquiring simple techniques to reduce human bias in both writing and speaking.

Good communicators don't need profanity to make meaning clear. Neither do good communicators need to fuel bias through words that exclude part of the population.

Could unbiased language achieve world peace, family harmony, and social justice? Possibly! And when a possibility exists, hope keeps us plugging on.

Refer to this guidebook when preparing business reports, ads, classroom assignments, news copy, sales literature, training material, customer letters, orders, Internet text, and when writing for newspapers, movies and television. Use it when dealing with people you believe are different from you. Talk to strangers (sorry, Mom); ask questions. There is no need to tiptoe around language to sincerely reach out to understand about "differences." You may find you can abolish labels to define Us and Them as you discover that we are all Us!

The bottom line (and this is only the introduction):

Don't assume, ask questions
Don't demean, listen
Don't stereotype
Don't accept labels
Do be respectful
Do find likenesses
Do appreciate the difference
Do be courteous
Do be aware!

If you come up with a problem of inclusive language that this book doesn't address, please send it to me in care of the publisher to receive a personal reply.

This book may be too upbeat for those who carry heavy loads in their hearts. For them, only a therapist's couch will be helpful. For those who recognize the humanity of us all, and the differences that add color and joy to daily lives, who want to improve the enjoyment of daily living, read on. Be patient with yourself, keep your mind wide open and look at those around you with a new unstained spotlight. What happens will be a pleasant surprise.

— Val Dumond

# 1

# Think Before You Use Words

## Why Discuss Words and Isms?

No one likes to feel left out. Yet, biased language that results from isms does exactly that — leaves out anyone who differs from the speaker or writer. Language is at the base of overcoming the idea of *Us* and *Them*. In this book, we'll focus on words such as: *open-minded, fair-minded, impartial, unbiased, bias-free, influential* — and *just.*

The Us and Them Thing is the attempt of self-aggrandizement that separates *Us* (who resemble one another in appearance and ideology) and Them (who appear different). It begins with gentle teasing and jokes, then becomes more abusive as language escalates, sometimes to the level of yelling and finger-pointing. The next level contains aggressive behavior that can grow into violence: hitting, shoving, and physical confrontation.

Define "physical confrontation" as the violence found in beatings, assault, murder and war. The pattern of escalation from *mis-speak* to *violence* is the same between individuals (friends, family members, strangers) or between nations.

It all begins with words.

Have we missed a chance at world peace by judging too harshly, criticizing too much. Are we Americans so eager to promote ourselves that we need to denigrate others?

Before moving into the "how to" sections, let's take a look at some of the idiosyncrasies of our crazy (American) language.

## Making Judgments

In all forms of communication, the first thing we do is make judgments, good, bad and innocuous. She's *blond* and *pretty*; he's *handsome*; she's *rich* and *tough*; he's *mean* and *scarred*; he is *short* and *dumb*; she's *angry*; he's *manipulative*; that one is *smart, tall, dark, poor, sensuous, delightful, nosy, boring, sexy*, and on and on.

The wonder of humans is our ability to talk to one another — face to face, by telephone, and by Internet. Each has its own special place in our communication system. The Internet provides a way to talk to someone from a distance, in a detached way. The telephone adds the flexes of the voice, provides intonations to stress ideas. Face to face talk adds the element of vision, where we can see each other.

The reason we discuss the subject of these judgments is that we often grab the first impression and stick it into a neat little pigeonhole, then label it, so we won't have to re-think the impression another time.

*She sounded old.*
*He used big words, must have an education.*
*Her spelling is atrocious; she must be stupid.*
*His tic says he's nervous, probably hiding something.*
*I can work with a woman who sounds like that.*

As we collect these judgments, we tend to stick with them. All blonds are ...; all tall men are ...; all those people are ...; and all of us are ....

Humanity — all of us — comes from a long line of descendents of the early survivors of some calamity that visited the earth thousands of years ago. Whether you accept the biblical notion or scientific discovery of the beginnings of humans, all of us are related. We are all humans, one species, the same kind of creature.

Yet we are barely able to tolerate our own families, never mind our neighbors, townspeople or the country next door. We fight (or want to fight) anyone who seems at all different from us — anyone who believes something different, who appears different, who speaks differently, or who owns more (or less)

## Noah's View

Take the story of Noah and his wife (I'd tell you her name, but the names of early women were not recorded).

Can you imagine what was sailing through Noah's mind as he perched atop that precarious precipice on Mt. Ararat? *Well now, God, you've had your bit of fun. You've virtually erased any life that pre-existed on earth. Now we're going to have to start over — from the beginning.*

Noah had two of everything, except humans; he had a family of those — a wife, three sons and their wives.

Now, the question must be raised: many generations later, how would Noah react to the way his descendents treat each other? We have divided ourselves into sects, tribes, colonies, nations, set up imaginary lines to keep apart from one another, believe that half of the population (gender-wise) has more rights than others. We disparage the shade of skin color, sanction those who grow old, but most of all, we set up ways to worship the Creator, then go after those who disagree? "Kids," the Creator might say, "Chill!"

than we do. We call them names, toss epithets at them, along with curses and innuendo.

How did we reach this place? And why is it important to understand the part that language plays in today's troubles? Perhaps we can best understand why adults act and react as we do by taking a look at children and how they learn.

## Children Learn Early

### Sticks & Stones

"Sticks and stones can break my bones, but words can never hurt me." Betcha your mother taught you that. Heck they can't! Words can hurt and harm and embarrass and demean. Words can break up long-time relationships. Words can demolish a child's self-image. Words can embarrass friends and business associates. Words can make others feel bad.

Let's go back to the beginning. Children learn to use words by mimicking what they hear. They try out new words on others, watch the reactions, and file away the information for later use. "I called him *stupid* and he hung his head." "She said I was *cute* and I felt tingly inside." "They shouted *nigger* and all those other people shouted back." "Teacher called out *troublemaker* and the child sat down."

In the words of the song about discrimination in James Michener's *South Pacific*, "you have to be carefully taught." Children are not born hating.

Hurtful words damage, embarrass and demean. When this happens, it's called discrimination, which finds many pathways to insinuate itself into modern culture. Ironically, the hurtful words are just as damaging to the speaker as to the listener.

Still, at its roots, discrimination is the *Us and Them Thing* (go ahead, trumpets! Ta-da!). Discrimination is the attempt to bolster our status by putting down others. Unfortunately, it usually begins with words, insinuation, and implication, then escalates to physical pushing, hitting and violence.

Remember the fourth grade? Or was it third? when you first noticed the Us/Them thing? That was about the time the boys in the Treetop Club began to tease the girls, who quickly formed the WHB (We Hate Boys) Club. Both clubs became tightly knit groups that banded together with

---

### Is Language Important?

Consider this: by the time a child is in high school, they've heard from adults the words *no, don't,* and *you can't* more than 50,000 times. In abusive families where the abuse is with words rather than fists, that number may be doubled, and include phrases such as *you'll never amount to anything, you're no good,* and *you're bad.* Is it any wonder that children grow up with low self-esteem and a tendency to repeat those words to those around them?

---

extensive rules of secrecy and belonging. These clubs were the precursors of all the grownup clubs people belong to. Perhaps this is a human thing that requires seeking others of our own kind to contrast those of another kind.

## Win / Lose

The U.S. is a nation of competitors — in education, lifestyle, business, and all of life (witness the plethora of record books and television game shows). Americans love to compete — and win. Who can throw the ball the farthest, fastest, highest? Who can hit the ball into a hole in the fewest possible strokes? Who can bear the most children? Whose kids become the highest paid professionals? Who can sit on a pole for the longest time? Who can teeter-totter the longest? Who has the biggest body parts? Who can survive the treachery of other "players"?

The win-lose competitiveness becomes "I'm better than you," or "I have to show you I'm better." Someone wins, someone loses! While winning feels great, it becomes necessary to look at how the winning is done, its fairness — level playing field, equal competitors — and the effect on the *loser*. Even the term *loser* contains remnants of "I'm not good enough," or "I'm not as good as the winner." What is wrong about being proud to be the second best? What is wrong about being the second fastest, strongest, prettiest, smartest person in the world? Or the third? Or in the top 100? Or even the top 100,000?

Americans compete in everything, even in the arena of length of life: "I'm much older than you." "Oh yeah? Well, I'm 68." "Ha! I'm 71!" "Hey, my dad lived to be 98!" "I've already outlived my siblings." "My mom lived to be 100." "Well, mine lived to be 101!"

How about considering democracy as a win-win way of life? How about finding ways to overcome the need to win at all costs? When someone wins, someone loses, whether competing in athletics, love, war, politics or age.

All living beings are created equal. It's the humans who insist on arranging them in a hierarchy of value — with humans on top. Then these brainy humans add layers to separate each other! — by gender, age, race, class, and nationality, to name a few.

## Is This Subject Important?

The *Us and Them Thing* refers to the tendency of humans to look at themselves as *Us* and others as *Them*. Not only do these terms divide people, they cause deep irreparable harm. Consider the *Us and Them* mind set that lies beneath the turmoil in practically every country in the world, including and especially, the United States of America.

The Us and Them mind set that becomes political, religious or racial often turns into violence and ultimately war. *"You don't believe the way I do (or look the way I do), therefore, I'm going to attempt to either convince you my way is better or eliminate you."* or *"If you don't agree with me, you must be against me."* Does this sound familiar? Take a long look at any of the world's dictators over the years who have spouted these or similar words.

Most who use (or misuse) the language don't realize they are doing so. These are the reasons to be bothered by the meanings of words — as a parent, communicator, business person, or citizen in a society that supposedly recognizes the equality of people with varying shades of skin color, religious backgrounds, financial status, sexual identity, age, or disability.

## Political Correctness

When change is imminent, discussion takes place and all too often results in requests for legislation to cure society's ailments. Following society's turmoil of the latter 20th century, legislation attempted to rein in *discrimination* against certain groups of people. Then came the formidable term, "Political Correctness." And the deep confusing pit began to be dug.

How are "groups" defined? How are lines drawn around differences? Which differences?

Woman: *Don't call me girl; I am woman; pay me a wage compatible with men.*

Man: *Don't blame me for holding open a door for you.*

Less-educated: *Don't call me dumb!*

Over-educated: *Don't blame me for being smart.*

Jew: *Don't expect me to be helpless outdoors.*

Irish: *Don't call me a lush.*

Indian: *Don't call me lazy.*

Southerner: *Don't make cracks about hillbillies.*

Westerner: *Hey, I don't even own cattle.*

Over-55: *Don't think my life is over.*

Teenager: *Don't think I don't know what's going on.*

*...and on and on.*

As one training session instructor put it sarcastically: "We're not using PC anymore. We're learning cultural sensitivity. And we're going to learn to be sensitive or I'll kill you!"

Political correctness doesn't work. When government and business set up guidelines as to who can say what, when and to whom, controls are impossible. Thought and language must not be legislated, monitored, policed, or adjudicated.

There are better ways to face off discrimination. They are: Respect and Courtesy.

The principles for addressing discrimination

> ### Discrimination
> A dictionary definition of *discrimination*: "an unfair word, act or policy stemming from prejudice." Or: "to influence in a particular, typically unfair direction." There are other words that are similar: *partial, biased, unfair, closed-minded* — and *unjust.*

are the same in all forms, and can be applied in equal ways. Discrimination is discrimination, whether it's aimed at the disabled, short or tall people, fat or skinny folks, in-laws, bosses, political parties, the mentally ill — in short, anyone who isn't like *Us.*

The challenge of "getting along," has always been an uphill struggle for humans. People come to America to be free — free to worship, free to pursue livelihood, free to think and express themselves, free to manage their lives and raise their families. Ironically, some discover a kind of division that can isolate and confine as much as any tyrannical political regime. And that division begins with labels — *just words.*

How community relationships reached the place where humans constantly try to separate into Treetop and WHB Clubs is not much of a mystery. *We* provides power against *Them.* Listen to the words: *we* and *them.* Feel the sense of these words. Americans are joiners; we like to belong, from the earliest years when we had treehouse clubs right through Rotary International. We like to write rules that include *Us* and exclude *Them*.

Writing or speaking so that you won't needlessly exclude or provoke any of your audience need not be difficult. What follows are just a few ideas to keep in mind when putting words together.

## Bigotry

*Bigotry* indicates "a strong partiality for one's own group (religion, race, age, class or politics) and is intolerant of those who differ." *American Heritage Dictionary* points out that the word *bigot* was used by the French as a term of abuse for the Normans, but not in a religious sense. Later, the word, or one like it, was used abusively in French for members of a Catholic lay sisterhood, and came to mean "excessively devoted or hypocritical." *Bigot* was first recorded in English in 1598 with the sense "a superstitious hypocrite."

We each have our own pets — peeve and otherwise — likes and dislikes. We also have our own ways of describing other people. Don't expect to please all people with your words. Talk it out. Dissention and personal opinion render discussions lively, even entertaining. People don't all think alike; you can't expect them to. Diversity and discussion — that's the beauty of the challenge of language.

Some common words that we use without thinking may be volatile. Consider:

*Indian giver*
*A Chinaman's chance*
*Jew them down in price*
*Pagan, crone, witch ...*
*Free, white and 21*
*Every American man is guaranteed his rights*

*College girls don't know much about mankind.*
*Nigger toes (Brazil nuts)*
*Eenie-meenie-minee-mo...*
*Another redskin bit the dust*
*Stoic as a cigar store Indian*

Sometimes when words such as these are used "because we've always used them," they pass unnoticed. Sometimes. Perhaps it's time to pay attention and become cognizant of the ways that words affect others. "I *protest* what you think; I *affirm* what I think" is the way it was voiced in a song by Peter, Paul and Mary.

Achieving inclusive language in daily communication may require some effort at first. But like most newly learned skills, it becomes easier as new habits begin to form. Soon you will be able to spot sexism, ageism, classism and racism in the communication of others as easily as you avoid it in your own.

As you become aware of language and how it reflects more than the surface definition, you will realize how important meanings are to all those who read and hear your words. Moreover, your awareness of language is guaranteed to improve the accuracy and effectiveness of your words — both written and spoken.

# 2

# Words! Image! Action!

## The Power of Inclusive Language
## Words — Attitude — Behavior

Words label, provide messages underneath the words, and often have dual meanings. Attitudes grow from words and group people together. Attitudes provide instant identification and are often based on perceptions of others. Behavior grows from attitudes, and often belittles, demeans, repeats messages from the past, and … can grow into violence.

Language evolves through all those stages: from words to attitudes to behavior. As Anonymous put it: "Graffiti is a terrorist attack in the larval stage." What evolves can be butterflies or mosquitoes.

What some think of as the War of Words, can quite literally happen. When the words of a family get out of hand, when school children's taunts escalate, when the words of diplomats and world leaders waver and grow aggressive, actual wars can be set off. The wilder the words, the more belligerent the attitudes, and the more violent the resulting actions.

Americans live in a diverse nation based on democracy, which recognizes the principles of social equality and respect for the individual. America was established on

11

the principle of freedom and rights for everyone. We are all immigrants; we all come from somewhere else. Even those we call Native Americans found their way here from somewhere else.

Language directly affects behavior. Language that disparages women becomes demeaning to half the population and therefore is connected to violence against women. Language that demeans people according to their skin color or family heritage demeans everyone and can escalate to violence against anyone. Language that diminishes those in a particular age group or economic level or physical identification, also diminishes everyone; we all pass through many groups on our way through life.

> # Words of War!
>
> War is the process of turning "the other" into an object in order to rationalize the killing that is inevitable in times of conflict. "As we denigrate the other and dehumanize the other, what we're doing linguistically is turning the other, the opponent — the enemy, if you want to call them that — into objects," claims Chris Hedges, noted war correspondent with the *New York Times*. "We do that first through language, then we do that quite literally by turning them into corpses."

Look, for example, at the evidence that substantiates the connection between verbal teasing of school children and the resulting violent behavior. Every child undergoes, to some degree, intimidation and humiliation as part of the public school process. The extreme involves a bully who terrifies another child with promises of pain if the child complains. But make no mistake, children who are taunted suffer from the daily degradation.

Repetition of abusive language is what makes it deadly. A social group of youngsters can exclude another child from their group for no better reason than the child is not as healthy or as wealthy or as well dressed as the group is. Later, the outcast may drive a different kind of car or hold (or not hold) a college degree. For whatever reason, the Us and Them thing has separated someone. And one day that separation could lead to physical action, whether mere pushing or fisticuffs or a bloody beating.

Or consider when marital abuse escalates from verbal abuse to physical violence, from put-downs to knock-downs. When governments use words as instruments of hate, you can be sure hate will turn the words into rocks, then swords, then guns, then bombs, then....

## Words Are Symbols

Words can be defined in two ways: 1) the dictionary way, a flat out description of an object or action, or 2) the conceptual way, an interpretation by the listener according to experience and training. The dictionary way is called denotative; the conceptual way is connotative.

Words are symbols. Words represent things. Some of the things are objects; others are concepts. A word like *cup* represents an object that generally is recognized as a receptacle. We can see it, touch it, pick it up or break it. We can describe its appearance. It can have many shapes, forms, and colors, but it usually serves the same function (some cups hold pencils).

A word like *freedom*, on the other hand, represents an idea, a concept. Its interpretation relies on the experience and beliefs of the interpreter (listener). We cannot see it, touch it, or pick it up. A reader or listener relies on their own meaning. Many listeners will interpret a word with their own versions, which can sometimes be negative; freedom may be a concept that is frightening or threatening to some people. Consider the shades of the following:

"I am *free* of my parents. Whee! Now I can do as I please."

"I want to be *free* of the daily beatings."

"Let me be *free* to make my own choices."
"If I were free, I'd have to earn my own living."
"When I'm *free* of these chains, I'll..."
"What a joy to be *free* of that desk for a week."

Have you ever heard yourself lament, "I know what I want to say, I just don't know how to say it"? Everyone sometimes experiences this loss of words. You see an image that you can't attach words to. While you may not be sure which comes first, the chicken or the egg, you do know about images and words. Images precede words, in civilization as well as in daily communications.

Do you know why you find it difficult to remember things in your life before about the age of three? That is because in those infant years, you did not use words; you relied on images.

You can close your eyes and possibly recall the taste of the bottle against your tongue, the light coming through a window at naptime, the discomfort of a wet diaper. But since you weren't relying on words (just cries and coos), it is difficult now to describe those sensations.

When words are spoken, the potential is there for at least three sets of interpretations to be attached to them. 1) The meaning that the speaker attaches to the image being defined; 2) The meaning given by the listener according to experience and understanding; and 3) The dictionary meaning.

The dictionary meaning is the general agreement about what a word means according to people in the language business. The *dictionary-says* definitions (which can reflect the experience of the dictionary writer / editor as well as common usage) gives a standardized meaning for most words. (Occasionally, however, a word is used that is not found in the dictionary but still carries a sensory meaning. Does that make four interpretations?)

## Words Are Tools

Experts guess there are nearly a million or so words in the English/American language, and that of these an average educated adult uses about 2,000. Of these, about 500 words carry more than 14,000 meanings, which says that most of the words we regularly use have multiple meanings. Some words are given as many as 100 meanings (consider: *put, take, get, do, make,* and *go*). It is no wonder that "average educated" adults find difficulty in transferring definitions of meanings to each other.

Now add to the above statistics the wildness of language brought about by the advent of the computer and the Internet. Words, symbols, letters, and smiley faces : )! Do you begin to perceive the dilemma of communication?

How does this affect the isms in our language?

Most of the English language was developed and defined by men. Male scholars developed the first recorded languages, translated words from other tongues, and then taught language skills, primarily to men. Women were not allowed to be educated in many early cultures — and some current ones. Little wonder that the language reflects a male point of view. Further, most of those men were white, since written language was developed mostly in Caucasian communities, and education was withheld from slaves in America.

Most people that we call *indigenous* or *native* are limited to spoken language, much of which is rapidly disappearing. Steven Pinker, noted linguistics professor at Massachusetts Institute of Technology, claims in his book, *The Language Instinct*, that no group of humans has been found without language. Many tribes have a utilitarian language that is completely oral — never written down. He also suggests that thousands of languages have developed and disappeared over time, no longer spoken by anyone. In North America, brave attempts are being made to restore disappearing languages of native people. The same is happening in Africa, Australia, and Asia and parts of Europe. But it seems to be a losing battle. Only a few aging people remember the fading languages, and young people seemingly move on to learn the "popular" languages of the world.

Words are the tools of civilization. Words are used to convey ideas of how people are expected to act, how they carry out what are considered stereotyped roles. Words can be used as weapons — as ways to hurt people, ways to inflict emotional harm through verbal abuse. Words can affect the emotional reaction of the listener in a subliminal, subconscious way, doing their damage over a period of time by reinforcing negative self-images.

## If We Were All Alike...

Generally, we are made uneasy by nonconformists, people who march to their own drummer. Still, shouldn't we be more uneasy with those who demand that we all become alike?

The idea of making all humans "the same" is the hideous nightmare lived out in science fiction literature that dresses everyone alike and designs identical bodies and faces. Which raises some questions: How would it feel if we were all alike? Who would we look like? Who would be the model for human life, or possibly "perfection." (The obvious answer is *Me!)*

In discussing likenesses and differences, it is important to recognize the extremes and seek the middleground. Somewhere in the middle is balance between recognizing how all humans are alike and appreciating the many ways we are different.

One of the purposes of this book is stated as: world peace. If this sounds far-fetched, consider the following very simple ideas:

What if ... Israel and Palestine recognized each other as two great cultures residing in one country, sharing their histories that go back millenia, and created a festival to celebrate their two proud heritages ...?

What if ... the Catholics and the Protestants of Ireland took time to realize both of their religions date back to the beginning of the Bible, and chose to honor both with shared holidays throughout the year ...?

What if ... the Middle-East Arab nations realized their many great tribes date back to the beginning of time — all of them — and enjoyed each others festivals of celebration and blessed each other's survival in a world rapidly trying to erase differences ...?

What if ... the people of the United States took a look around and said, Hey, we have the whole world right here in one great nation? Aren't we fortunate!

## A Global Village

The Global Village has been described by various people as a strange mixture of human beings. The following profile of such a village of 100 people is attributed to World Teach, a nonprofit organization based at Harvard University which sends volunteers overseas to teach in developing countries.

A village of 100 people who represent the Earth's total population would look like this:

57 Asians
21 Europeans
14 North and South Americans
8 Africans
70 would be people of color, 30 white
30 would be Christian, 70 of other faiths
50% of the wealth would be in the hands of six people, all citizens of the United States
70 would be unable to read
80 would have substandard housing
One would have a university education.

The theme of this book is clear: Respect and Courtesy — Respect for a difference of opinion, Respect for the individual who expresses it, and Courtesy with fellow travelers on this planet. Keep those powerful words in mind as you write and talk, and your message will be easier to understand.

If you want an exercise in the power of words and a demonstration of how they lead to attitudes which, in turn, lead to behavior, read over "Herstory" in the Appendix. You may be in for a surprise — whether you are male or female, have dark or light skin, are under or over the median age line. This brief essay is a strong example of what words can do.

World Peace? Why not!

# 3

# Habits Are Hard To Break

## Alternative Choices

Many cultural habits contribute to the isms in American language. Habits are picked up from family, from school — from learning to talk by listening to the world around us. Most of the time these language habits result in automatic usage; we don't think about the meanings of the words we choose.

One such habit, the indiscriminate tendency to add *man* to many words, is one unfortunate idiosyncrasy of English, as in words such as *salesman, chairman, journeyman, spokesman* and *fireman*.

Then there are the words referring to separate cultures. Words like "us" and "them" are used casually when referring to people of other racial or national backgrounds, or what are perceived as "other" backgrounds.

Youngsters think *whippersnapper* and *codger* are clever words for those in that *other* age bracket. Just as many adults group those youngsters together as *teeny-boppers* or *rappers*.

Habits are difficult to break — but not impossible. Many of our linguistic habits have been developed through centuries of repetition. Sexist language is the

19

result of the men who steered the development of language. Cultural language has become deeply ingrained by the conquesting traits of these same men. Racist language comes from differences in appearance. Ageist language comes from the natural process of youth fearing age, and age regretting the loss of youth.

How often we hear the words, "But we've always done it that way!" Well, in the language business, these words do not apply — justly. Language changes with the times. And the bad habits of language can be changed with a bit of awareness and a whole lot of compassion. How? Reconstruct language to include women. Recognize the contributions of other cultures. Accept the foibles of youth as *hope for the future* and the frailties of age as *wisdom*.

Some habits have become part of our American language. Consider each of the following from the "other" point of view.

## Age

For some reason, newspapers (especially) feel the need to discover and print the ages of everyone they write about. While it may seem to be important in the event of certain newsworthy items, it may be unnecessary in the long run. Age is important in obituaries, since they tend to review a person's life; age would be less important in a feature story about the special talents of an artist or business executive.

With increasing awareness of age in this culture, the importance of respecting each other regardless of age becomes more important. Everyone is growing older. Wasn't it journalist Andy Rooney who noticed wryly that "all those youngsters will be in our place one day." As for youth? Ah, ain't it grand! (As long as it lasts.) You hear youths say, "Old age? It won't happen to me!" However, given half a chance, it does.

The obvious language problem involving age would be referring to older people as *golden agers, senior citizens, old fogies, codgers,* and so on. Some older people object to these terms; others embrace them. After all, there are some benefits to being identified as a "senior citizen" (in discounts for admissions and sales). But oh, the teeth grating among many elders when so addressed.

Young people too in recent decades have been lumped together according to generations. Following the Great Depression generation and The War generation, have come the Baby Boomers, Generation X, and of late, Generation Y. This may be a handy way to rank people of a certain age, but before you do, check with them to see if they are thrilled with the label. (One wonders at the implication that when we reach Generation Z, we have come to the end of the line!)

The best way to refer to people of any age is as people.

## Animals

As long as we personify animals in cartoons, advertisements, and stories, be aware of the biological fact that all animals are not male, nor are all animals female.

While this may seem obvious, habitual usage seems to give male gender to the birds of the air, animals of the woods, and fish in the sea. Some of these habits have caused some ludicrous and inaccurate sentences, such as the following:

*The cow had a fly on his tail.*

*The doe had a frightened look in his eye.*

*The two-year-old mare won his first race by six lengths.* (Even worse) *The mare won his maiden race by six lengths.*

Do not assume that an animal is male or female unless words makes this clear or the animal's gender is otherwise specified (the buck raised his eyes, the turtle laid her eggs). Too many textbooks, as well as story books, abound with such statements as these:

> *The white-tailed deer lives in his woodland habitat.*
> *When a seagull searches for his dinner, he flies*
>     *toward the fishing boats.*
> *All of the pig is used commercially, even his tail.*
> *The turtle's shell is his home.*

The female turtle also lives in a shell home!

## Bitches, Bastards and Whores

Cuss words have entered daily language to a place where they're used without thinking. Let's take a moment to consider the meanings behind some of them. Did you notice that the word "bitch" derives its meaning from motherhood? that "bastard" and the phrase "born out of wedlock" refer to a child? Whether or not a child's parents have gone through some ritual does not determine a child's worth. Is this any way to treat a mother?

---

### *A Note To Filmmakers —*

Producers of nature documentaries, movies, advertisements and commercials need to look closely at manuscript texts to ferret out erroneous animal gender identifications. In the English language, it is perfectly acceptable to refer to animals with the neuter pronoun *it*. Remember that the deer in the forest, rabbits under the trees, eagles in the air, chickens in the yard, and dogs in the pound all share sexual distinctions, just like people. All species come in two genders, female and male. Use *he* when referring to male animals, *she* for female animals, and *it* when you don't know the animal's gender or when gender is not a factor.

Animal terms when applied to people can demean through sexual implication, as in *bull session* or *hen party*. It is unlikely you can avoid all such terms, but at least be aware of how they are used. And when you recognize the sexism in them, you'll also become aware of the effect on those receiving the innuendoes.

---

Words such as "slut, whore, harlot, strumpet, hustler," are reflections on women who choose to sell their bodies to men who are willing to buy them. It's a trade that seems to have a place in our world — since time began. To judge a woman who makes this choice is unjust. Today's women who prostitute themselves are called "working women" or "sex workers" and usually are the ones arrested. Men, once called "johns" or "tricks," generally remain anonymous. What's wrong with this picture?

> ## Black + White = US
>
> Population experts predict that in two or three more generations, maybe sooner, the distinctions between white and black people, between white and Asian, between white and Latino, will be blurred to a point where it will be difficult to identify people by race or skin color. [Even in writing that paragraph, the urge was strong to place quote marks around "white" and "black."]

## Census

Perhaps we ought to ask the question "Who are you?" rather than "What are you?" It would certainly make life easier for people who can barely go back two generations to discover their cultural "identities," or care to.

Why, for instance, does the government need to know one's "race?" Much of our outer appearance is subject to change anyway: we color our hair, grow and style it, haunt tanning salons, correct our shapes and sizes with surgery, and alter ourselves in unnamable ways. Will the day come when we disregard the shade of skin color, amount or color of hair, size of waist or nose as relevant to how people treat each other?

Perhaps racial identification history made a turn in the road when golfer Tiger Wood described his background as "Thai-African-Chinese-American Indian." On most census

## Census & Blood

There was a time when governments felt it needed to know "if there was a single drop" of certain kinds of blood in an individual. (Remember those dreadful designations on early census forms: quadroon and octoroon?) We now know that all blood contains similar components that cannot designate nationality nor race. We *can* designate only Types A, B, AB or O. No longer can we claim, "There is not a drop of Dutch blood in me," (nor Indian, nor African, nor royal, nor blue, nor Negro). We cannot change our blood by moving to another country, nor can we change our blood by identifying our ancestors. That's not quite right; we *can* discover blood type and DNA type (which still does not relate in any way to skin color).

The Census Bureau now offers "multiracial" as a label choice. About time. How is it possible for some to distinguish between Hispanics, Mexicans, Puerto Ricans, Cubans, Latinos, Spanish? Between Jamaican, African, Honduran or Georgian? Between Laotian, Cambodian, Vietnamese, Tongonese or Malasian? Or German, Irish, or French? Or Canadian?

Skin shading no longer is a reliable designation of race or nationality. Why should it be of concern to anyone?

forms, however, he probably is designated as "black." We've come so far, but we still can go farther in breaking down the barriers, the mythology and the distinction of race.

## Complexion

How often have you heard someone say, "She was dark-complected"? Not only is this term a grammatical atrocity, (the word is *complexioned*), but it can be construed with racial implications. Look around you. Can you possibly accurately categorize people by their skin tone? Or hair color? Humans are made of skin in colors ranging from pale cream to walnut-brown, and hair described as lemon yellow, orange, red, brown, black, gray and white and all the shades in between. (If you have doubts, check out the hair color shelf at the pharmacy near you.)

When it is necessary to describe skin and hair color, it usually is in connection with identification.

Use skin and hair color carefully, without alluding to the trite referral to Asians as yellow, Indians as red, Africans as black, Europeans as white, and middle-easterners and Latinos as brown. This just doesn't work any more and is unacceptable in a nation made up of people with mixed family trees that cover the world.

*Racial profiling* is a habit that has developed from the years following desegregation. More recently, the term has been used to identify anyone of color or ethnic background — from Mideast Arabs to Asians. It means that we often attach an entire culture as well as a national and racial background to the color of someone's skin or the configuration of their appearance. Making generalities such as this can lead to implications that are either demeaning or discriminating, and most likely are inaccurate.

Prediction: In a few years, applications and census forms will eliminate references to racial data.

## Dwarfs, Midgets, and Munchkins

Approximately 24,000 people are members of Little People of America, an organization that represents about one in a thousand who are born smaller than most babies and who do not grow as large as the general population.

Danny Woodburn, a character actor, asks that people regard each other for who they are rather than how they look. He has stated, "I don't want to be seen as a little person actor or a dwarf actor. I am a character actor; that's what I studied to do."

Woodburn contends that we celebrate diversity in art, music, and intellectual endeavors, but we don't celebrate the diversity of physical appearance. "We want people to look the same," he said. "Do we change society's misperceptions or do we change our appearance?"

A huge cosmetic industry and an equally huge plastic surgery industry have grown up by touting the belief that changing appearance changes "the person." However, some physical traits are less simple to change: a short person cannot add height; a tall person cannot cut it back. Each human has a body to use for a few decades — and there is not a one-size-fits-all policy.

Woodburn suggests that society begin to change itself by shouting, "Look at me! I can do anything. And I'm little" (big, tall, fat, skinny, dark, light, mis-shapen, blind...), "so back off!"

## Disabilities

Notice that it was only after legal intervention that consideration was given to areas which were inaccessible to wheelchairs. What ever made us think that people in wheelchairs didn't care to go to the movies? or a favorite restaurant? or a swimming pool? or shopping? or a sports arena?

Break the habit of looking at wheelchair occupants as "damaged." Many people are grateful for a wheelchair that gives them the ability to move around. Damaged legs or spine doesn't preclude damaged brains. Consider Christopher Reeve and Stephen Hawking — both have made major contributions to the world from their wheelchairs.

## First Names

When writing about people (for a newspaper or newsletter, for instance), use the first name of the individual only if first names are used for everyone; otherwise use last names and titles. It is belittling to call a woman by her first name while using the title and last name for a man. Consistency is the guideline.

Do not use: *President and Bess Truman*
Use: *President Truman and Mrs. Truman*
or *Harry and Bess Truman*

Use:
> *Governor Locke and Governor Ray*

or
> *Gary Locke and Dixy Lee Ray*

but not
> *Governor Locke and Dixy Lee Ray*

When *both* married partners share titles (as with doctors), use their titles equally: Dr. Doe and Dr. Doe, or Drs. Doe (not Dr. Doe and Mrs. Doe, or Dr. and Mr. Doe).

Often older people are addressed as Mr. or Ms. while younger people's first names are used. This is another habit that needs to go. Use either all first names or all titles of address and last names.

How often in a professional's office will the professional be addressed as Doctor or President or Captain, while the non-professional is addressed by a first name. When a doctor calls you by your first name, respond by using the doctor's first name.

> **NOTE:** In emergencies medical personnel
> ask your name to help with both the trust
> level and the response to treatment. You
> don't need to know the physician's names —
> first or last — but they need to know yours,
> and quickly.

## Founding Fathers, Brothers, and BOMFOG

This country's pioneers, founders, trailblazers, and innovators were not all men. Historians have overlooked women in the wording and connotations of those who came before. *Founding fathers* can be changed easily to *forebears*. Pioneers usually are defined in masculine terms, when facts clearly indicate women were pioneers too.

Even further back, predecessors are represented as *cavemen*. Consider Cro-Magnon Man, Neanderthal Man, and so on. Biologically, there had to be cavewomen or you wouldn't be here now.

*Brotherhood* is another word that does not include women. Just as *sisterhood* does not include men. The word *kindred* better expresses the idea of the unity of people; it includes both women and men. *Siblinghood* might be stretching things too far.

BOMFOG is translated to stand for "Brotherhood of Man / Fatherhood of God," a term that sounds very noble until you think about all the people who are left out.

As for a definition of God or Allah, let's leave that to the innermost surprise of each individual. How religion became so constricted, confining, cramped, narrow, small, and closed spiritually, while growing so large and power-ful structurally, remains an enigma. The spirit, after all, remains the greatest mystery of all, a strong, delicate truth that has its power in its wonder.

Try using words such as: Almighty, Great Spirit, Cre-ator, Supreme being, or Omnipotent being.

## Guys ...

The second most insidious word that has come to be habitually misused is the word "guy." Use of *guy* will always carry a subliminal meaning of "male." Guys are men. Yet, current usage has switched from referring to all of humanity as "men" by substituting the word "guys."

It becomes ludicrous when a clerk or server ap-proaches a group of mature women and asks, "How are you guys today?" Apparently, this is a cultural habit that has grown over the last few decades. Still, it is a habit that can be broken — simply by becoming aware of it.

## ...and Girls

*The most* insidious word in misuse today is "girls." Notice that women who are considered to be of "lower rank" are called *girls*: prostitutes, models, female actors, store clerks, even secretaries. What is more condescending is the trend toward eliminating the term "secretary" by bumping it up to "administrative assistant," then still referring to those women as "girls."

Much could be achieved in the field of respect for women if the term "girls" could be confined to young pre-teen females. Remember that girls are young females (usually under the age of 14). As girls grow into their teens, they become young women; address them that way. Notice how many insecure men tend to refer to women as *girls*. It seems difficult for some men to acknowledge the power of the word *women*. (Even women U.S. senators are often referred to as *girls*. But the most illustrative example is provided by fathers of grown daughters. How few fathers can allude to their daughters as women!)

A note about older women who call themselves "the girls:" Most are close friends and address each other in a friendly "insider" way. However, don't interpret that to mean that they welcome being called *girls* by others. Additionally, there are women who try to keep themselves young by referring to themselves as *girls*. Be assured this is the result of generations of humans referring to women as *girls*, and of women accepting that submissive second-place role.

This girl term also points up the tendency to favor young, nonthreatening women over mature confident women in today's society. This may be the most difficult habit to break!

Insider terms are a facet of the Us and Them Thing that propels the energy. Certain groups (businesses, pro-fessions, organizations, social clubs) develop languages of their own — to make it difficult for "outsiders" to pen-etrate the inner sanctum, thus furthering the distinctions between Us and Them.

Familiar words are often used by insiders in a way difficult to understand by outsiders. People of ethnic groups, families, people of similar age, race, or gender, feel comfortable with words that they wouldn't accept from others. Kate Hepburn can call Hank Fonda "you old poop," Eddie Murphy can greet IceT as "nigger," Frank Sinatra can refer to Dean Martin as "dago," and Oprah can call Aretha "girl," because these terms are meant in an insider friendly way. However, the same words spoken by an outsider wield a very different, very negative power.

## Life Roles

People sometimes are expected to assume roles in life according to their gender or age, rather than according to abilities and desires as individuals. It begins when girls grow up playing with dolls and learning to be passive, accommodating, and nurturing — housekeeper, wife, caretaker, mother and generally submissive human being — and boys grow up with baseball bats, trucks, and scooters, learning roles that are active and commanding — father, protector, wage earner, and generally aggressive human being.

If you doubt this, watch television commercials with the sound turned off; notice boys bouncing around while girls sit on the sidelines cheering them on, men driving sleek new cars with adoring women passengers, men digging up gardens and driving tractors while the women rock away on the porch (or bring them lemonade).

Psychology researchers are discovering that these tendencies are learned, that girls are taught to prepare for submissive roles by keeping quiet as youngsters. At the same time, boys are taught to prepare for aggressive roles by keeping active as children.

What if girls were given a rough-and-tumble childhood and boys a relaxing, inactive childhood? Would their adult roles be different than they are now? You bet, say many researchers. Not at all, say others. The ways to find out are almost impossible to control. Talk to women who have reached positions of power and ask about the way they were brought up. They'll readily explain that their parents did not let them believe there were restrictions about what a girl could achieve.

Toy makers are busy designing toys for children, toys that are attractive equally to boys and girls whether they are active or inactive children. Parents constantly debate the pros and cons of giving trains and basketballs to girls, dolls and tea sets to boys.

Meanwhile, children continue to read stories about males: Peter Rabbit, Harry Potter, Tarzan, Charlie Brown, Father Time. They observe holidays at school by coloring pictures of Santa Claus, Tom Turkey, St. Patrick, St. Valentine, and even Snoopy (boy dog) — all male figures.

Children's books lean towards male protagonists: *the boy and his dog, the boy and his wagon,* or *the boy and his friends.* Publishers are slowly *discovering* a whole new genre in books for girls.

As an eye-opening, exercise, re-read *Huckleberry Finn* as if the boy were a girl. Or read *Anne of Green Gables* as if she were a boy.

## Heroes Come In All Genders, Colors, Sizes

Heroes of our nation are depicted as men, beginning with George Washington, Father of Our Country, and moving forward. Actually, school history lessons begin with Amerigo Vespucci, Christopher Columbus, Leif Erickson, Miles Standish, Capt. John Smith, John Paul Jones, Patrick Henry, Benjamin Franklin, and on and on. It would seem there were few women alive during those early centuries. Dictionaries define hero as *"1) a man of distinguished courage or ability, admired for his brave deeds. 2) a man*

## Hero Was A Woman!

The dictionary describes a "heroine" as a female who acts bravely, like a (male) hero.

The irony is that the word hero comes from the Greek priestess of Aphrodite named Hero, the woman who loved Leander. When Leander was drowned trying to swim the Hellespont to be with her, Hero threw herself into the sea. Hero was a woman!

*who is regarded as having heroic qualities. 3) the principal male character in a story, play, etc. 4) a man of great strength and courage, favored by the gods and in part descended from them, often regarded as a half-god and worshiped after his death."*

—Webster's New World Dictionary, 3rd College Edition

Where does that leave women? With *heroine!* Here's a definition of "heroine" from the same dictionary: *"a girl or woman of outstanding courage, nobility, etc., or of heroic achievements."*

—Webster's New World Dictionary, 3rd College Edition

Who can name Noah's wife? or his daughters-in-law? Yet those women are purported to be the mothers who birthed civilization!

As for people of color, history lessons barely mention Frederick Douglas or Harriet Tubman, or other blacks who helped found this country. It took the advent of "Black History" to recognize the contributions of early blacks to the founding and development of the United States.

One of the best history lessons can be found on the comic pages in February, during Black History Month, when the characters of "Jump Start," written by Robb Armstrong, try to stump each other with information about significant people of color who have been overlooked by "white" history books.

Who can name American Indians in history, other than Geronimo, Pocahontas and Sacajawea (thank you, Mr.

Disney)? Who can name the innumerable courageous people of color who helped build this country?

## Masculine / Feminine

Traits and qualities of humans are found in both sexes. *Strong* and *brave* do not necessarily mean "masculine," nor are *tender* and *nurturing* automatically feminine traits. Beware of the temptation to use gender-linked adjectives to describe characteristics shared by all humans. When inclined to use a feminine or masculine symbol, look for a better image — inclusive rather than stereotypical, a symbol that includes rather than stereotypes.

And please, stay away from comparing genders: a baseball player (male) who throws "like a girl" or an executive (female) who conducts a meeting "like a man."

Avoid the trap of giving gender to inanimate things. Boats, cars and machines are things and require the pronoun "it."

Implications of unpredictability or treachery that accompany such words as *witch, Mother Nature, mother of change*, and *weak sex* give unfair meanings to femininity. Likewise, words like *master, father,* and *patron* cast implied masculine meanings of leadership and power. Be aware of the effects of habitual use of these and similar terms to imply gender.

Unfortunately, dictionaries contribute to the misuse of many adjectives. One defines *female* as an adjective meaning "womanish, or unmanly." *Male*, on the other hand, is never defined as being "mannish, or unwomanly."

## Members of Congress

Have you noticed that some of our Congress*men* are women? Women make up less than 15% of the total members of Congress (79 out of 535 in the 109th Congress (2005). That represents an increase of six women in the

House and no changes in the Senate. The nation continues to count women as 52% of the population. (Meanwhile in Iraq, women held 25% of the seats in the new
Congress in August 2004.)

When writing to your Congressional Representative
about this disparity in representation, be sure you use the
appropriate title. Read through the Constitution of the
United States and you will not find a single reference to
these representatives as *Congressmen.* What better authority could you follow?

The correct title for a member of the U.S. Senate is
*Senator.* A member of the other legislative branch is a
*Member of the House, a Congressional Representative,* or a
*Member of Congress.*

The law remains dim on treatment of sexual preference, and the U.S. Constitution remains the only one in
the world that does NOT include women. Men have
controlled education and government for millennia; is it
any wonder women have a rough time claiming their
space?

## Patron / Matron

The words *patron* and *matron* are not equal terms.

Traditionally, people who donate to charities are
referred to as *patrons.* The word comes from the Latin
*pater* (father) which means "benefactor or protector."
When this word is used to confer the meaning of benefactor, the fatherly connotation is implied.

Instead, use these words: *sponsor, donor,* or *supporter.*

In the same manner, a *patronizing* remark is one that
condescends (there's the father scolding and diminishing
the child). Stay away from *patronizing* as a substitute for
words that mean authority or protection. As a test, ask
yourself if you could substitute the word *matron.* Now
there's a whole new meaning!

[Isn't it interesting that *matron* is often used to mean a supervisor of women, sometimes in prison. A *patron* would never consider this job. Just as a *matron* may not be the best person to contribute to your favorite charity.]

## People With Disabilities

Myths abound concerning people with disabilities. In an effort to clarify, a brochure has offered "Tips For Disability Awareness."

Here are some excerpts:

—Adjusting to a disability requires adapting to a lifestyle, not "bravery and courage."

—A wheelchair is a vehicle, a personal assistance device that enables someone to move around. Many people use wheelchairs for reasons that have nothing to do with lingering illness.

—Not all persons with hearing loss read lips.

—People who are blind do not automatically acquire "a sixth sense."

—People with disabilities are not necessarily more comfortable "with their own kind." New opportunities are opening to everyone to join society's mainstream.

—Many people with disabilities are quite independent. If you want to help someone with a disability, ask first if they need it.

—Most people with disabilities do not mind responding to a child's question.

—People with disabilities go to school, marry, work, have families, do laundry, grocery shop, laugh, cry, pay taxes, get angry, have prejudices, vote, plan, and dream.

—Speak up when negative words or phrases are used in connection with a disability.

(Write for your free copy of "Tips for Disability Awareness" provided by Easter Seals at: 230 West Monroe, Suite 1800, Chicago, IL 60606.)

## Person

The average person on the street is not necessarily a man. In fact, since half of the population actually are women (more than half when you look at the latest census), avoid using such terms as "man on the street" or "average man" unless you are referring to a specific man on the street or you are taking averages only among men. It's just as easy to talk about *people on the street, a person on the street, an average person,* or *a typical person.*

> ### Readerperson (?)
> Don't be in a hurry to substitute the word "person" every time you see the word "man." The results can become ridiculous. Of late, the world has been overcome with *spokespersons, chairpersons, statespersons,* even *musicpersons.* Look at how many specific words are available that will let you skip *person* whenever a confusion of gender exists.

Beware, however, of the connotations of the term *street people.* In current culture, this generally refers to the homeless. (Don't we have an interesting language?)

In the same way, hypothetical people are not always men. Textbooks are beginning to use inclusive language to present math and other examples:

Example:

S:  *If a man can jog three miles an hour, how long would it take him to jog six miles?*

N:  *If a jogger can run three miles an hour, how long would it take to jog six miles?*

It is not necessary to use *person* when you really mean a man. If you are talking about a man in sales, by all means call him a *salesman.* Similarly, if you are talking about a woman in sales, she is a *saleswoman.* But if you are talking about some unidentified person in sales, use *person,* or a more specific word, such as *clerk, agent, representative,* or any number of other accurate descriptive nouns.

Be sure that when you use *person*, it is to refer to an unidentified or non-gender-specific individual. Don't use *spokesman*, for instance, in reference to a man, and in the next breath use *spokesperson* to refer to a woman doing the same job. In that instance, she is a *spokeswoman*. The two of them can be called "speakers on behalf of the organization."

The word *person* needs to be neither ridiculously overused nor overzealously avoided.

## Sports

All baseball players are not men — nor are all athletic figures and sports players men. Sports is not an exclusively male domain (although many would prefer it that way).

Use either *male* or *female* baseball players when specifying certain gender-restricted players, or just use *baseball players* when referring to

> ### Playing is Business
> "Sports" connotes an atmosphere of games and fun and doing one's best. To see how that has been corrupted, look at the evolution of the Olympic Games, as well as commercial sports (how's that for an oxymoron?). Playing in the U.S. has become big business while our business has become a game. Who wins? Who loses? Us or Them?

people who play baseball. Will the time ever come when women and men will play on the same professional sports teams — baseball, basketball, football, soccer, squash, lacrosse …?

If you refer to sports people as either *Mr.* or *Ms.* for identification, do so equally for both men and women.
Example:
S: *O'Connor and Ms. Lloyd played in a mixed double.*
N: *Mr. O'Connor and Ms. Lloyd played in a mixed double.*
or *O'Connor and Lloyd played in a mixed double.*

Now a note about the names of some of those teams. Columnist Leonard Pitts Jr. devoted a column to this subject. He referred to the professional sports teams: Cleveland Indians, Atlanta Braves, Kansas City Chiefs, and the Washington Redskins, not to mention the myriad of high school teams with similar names. While the piece was aimed mainly at American Indians, he also mentioned the Fighting Irish, the Boston Celtics, even the Lucky Charms leprechaun and asked why Indians "pitch a fit about a handful of sports teams" while the Irish were not up in arms. "The answer," Pitts wrote, "is simple: It's easier to laugh when you're in on the joke, and Indian people are not. See, there's a crucial difference between the Irish and the Indians. The one was assimilated, the other decimated."

You can understand that the idea of a group of people being considered as mascots to commercial game players might be construed as belittling, insulting, even an unbearable attack upon their collective dignity.

## Subliminal Messages

Sexist language crops up through the subliminal meanings of certain cultural attitudes. The belief that women are passive and men are active is based on beliefs that certain words are more powerful than others.

Women may refer to a certain color as *lilac, violet, lavender, raspberry*, or *mauve;* men call it *purple.* Women use adjectives such as *little, really,* and *somewhat*, whereas men use direct words and avoid the diminishing ones. Women use more passive language; men use more direct terminology.

There are women who don't always regard themselves or their work seriously. You'll hear them downplay their activities by referring to "our little party," or "my little business." And it seems as if women are constantly apologizing, more so than men. Listen to conversations and learn who says "I'm sorry" and when they say it. Business people notice, for instance, that men seldom if ever apologize for being late to a meeting. Women always do.

A good example of a subliminal use of language is in a news report giving the scores for a state high school basketball tournament. The following girls' scores are given passively and negatively:

> *Central team lost to Midland School 87 to 77.*
> *Universal School was smothered by Adams 97 to 65.*

Conversely, the boys' scores are given actively and positively:
> *The Main Team won over the Majors 78 to 66.*
> *The Champs Team whipped the Scroungers 79 to 56.*

Probably the most deceptive use of subliminal language to undermine a particular group of people is the daily connection made between skin color and economic condition. Many believe that to be black is to be poor, and to be poor is to be of color. *Minorities* has become a hateful word used prolifically to imply poverty and ineptitude. The word has become a euphemism that many use to avoid indications of race or culture.

When women are included in the term *minorities*, a great misstatement of fact has occurred; women are a majority! Yet, the subliminal message remains when such terms are used.

## Try It Sometime

A woman recently was injured in an auto accident and had to use a wheelchair for a few days. She learned quickly of the way much of society discounts people in wheelchairs, sometimes not even noticing them.

Additionally, people who use wheelchairs are often coupled with words such as *crippled, disabled, deformed* and *disfigured*, as well as generally dismissed as being *incompetent*.

Try it sometime! Great books have been written by people who changed the shade of their skin to experience how it feels to belong to another race. They are astonished that an entire group of people can be singled out as having certain traits based on the color of their skin?

In some cultures, older people are esteemed for their longevity and wisdom, and young people are given encouragement and guidance. When people are by-passed or deemed invisible because of their age (whether young and inexperienced, or aged with wrinkled skin) a culture loses the strengths that could be used for the betterment of society.

While it may be difficult to experience the under-skin feelings of another, or the comprehension of another culture, it may be possible over a lifetime to experience the age thing, or the religion thing, or the disability thing. Fortunately, humans have an imagination and can sense what it's like to be someone else — if we try.

What is that venerable Indian adage about walking a mile in another's moccasins before making judgments? What a very wise suggestion!

## Women at Work

Think about that term, *working woman*. Is that a woman whose arms and legs are operative, whose head turns on its neck axis and who can smile and say Thank You?

Habit has provided the traditional role of woman as homemaker and principal parent. For too many years, the homemaker has been referred to as "only a housewife" or as a "non-working woman." Both usages are inaccurate. (Have you ever followed a homemaker around for a day?)

Homemakers, both male and female, work — sometimes harder than anyone else. Certainly longer (they don't punch time clocks). Neither do they receive paychecks.

Homemakers are doing important work that doesn't deserve the diminishing word *only*.

> **NOTE:** Isn't it strange that job categories are divided into "men's work" and "nontraditional work"? If you want to realize just how strange, consider "women's work" as opposed to "nontraditional work."

Do you assume that women are responsible for operating the home? Do you ask to speak to the "lady of the house"? When you're hungry, do you ask the woman for something to eat?

If so, you may need to look closer at what is happening around you. Some homes are being operated by men, often called "househusbands." Take care when sending a note home with a youngsters; don't address it to Mom. Or when you want the chief homemaker, the decision-maker, don't assume who this will be.

What about women who work outside the home (as well as in it)? Don't call them *working women, working wives,* or *working mothers.* No more than you would refer to men as *working men, working husbands* or *working fathers!* (In some areas, prostitutes are called "working women." "Women at work" or "hired women" might be fairer terms.)

Women who hold salaried jobs are businesswomen, sales representatives, doctors, salaried women, lawyers, clerks, administrators, or any number of other such job titles. The woman who holds a job at home (paid or otherwise) is a woman who works at home.

Be careful when using terms like *motherhood, fatherhood, parenting, homemaking, wife, husband, grandmother,* and *grandfather.* Are you using them accurately and appropriately? Is it necessary to specify personal family roles? Roles and societal word usage are changing. If one political candidate is referred to as a "grandmother of six," describe her opponent as a "grandfather of four."

## Habitual Phrases

Generalizing is another habit that gets people into trouble with misleading assumptions, such as:

*Most women*
*Just like a woman*
*Old wives' tale*
*A woman's place*
*Most men*
*Just like a man*
*A man's responsibility*
*Stupid kids*
*Doddering oldster*
*White master*
*Black slave*
*Asian musician*
*Jewish merchant*

Consider:
*The defendant's lawyer was a black woman, only 24.*

(The implications: *my, my, a woman! Not likely capable. A black, not likely educated. And young! Can't know anything. Imagine that — incredible!*)

Habits and habitual word usage are difficult to change and require both care and attention. Have fun spotting an inaccurate or ludicrous remark that won't stand up under scrutiny for specific meaning.

*"Did that salesgirl just call me 'honey'?"*
*"I'm not prejudiced; I have many black friends."*
*"It must be difficult to be handicapped?"*

*"Our target market is 18 to 45, but lots of older people are interested."*

*"We have many older people here; you guys are welcome too."*

*"That stupid little kid just cut me off in traffic!"*

Keep biased remarks out of your spoken language and away from appearing in your writing, business literature or correspondence. Keep them from leaving your mouth by checking temptation with the question, "Would this apply to the other gender, another race or age group?" "Is gender, race or age a necessary element?" "I didn't even see that driver; it could have been another senior like me."

> ### 50 Degrees of Separation
> Genealogy studies indicate that everybody on earth is related, with the distance between relationships no more than 50th cousin (and most not that distant). You only have to think about it for a moment and do the math. For instance, genealogists point out that about 102 people came to America on the Mayflower in 1620. One estimate of descendants numbers between 20 and 30 million. This means that a full 10 percent of the population in the U.S. today are related to each other by marriage or blood — from that small segment of "foreigners" alone.

Writers, check closely to be sure you are using words to the best of your ability, exactly, specifically, to give your readers the appropriate meaning you wish to convey and not the meaning they must work to decipher.

One minister sent out a newsletter containing the statement, "Only man can sin," to which more than one woman in the congregation breathed a sigh of relief.

Speakers and writers: assume not a darn thing about people based on what you see. Rich people can wear jeans and T-shirts; poor people can wear fancy clothes.

Wrinkled people can have creative ideas and short people can have senses of responsibility. People in wheelchairs have lost the function of their bodies, not their minds. People of color — that actually means all of us — have families, homes, businesses, interests, abilities, feelings, and habits.

In a nation founded on diversity, where immigrants rush to learn English as a new language, and where new Americans yearn to become "one of the family," it would seem fitting to teach students that "whatever their ethnic

## IN THE BEGINNING...

Recent studies in genetics and genealogy have turned up evidence that divisions by race are unfounded. Scientists who study the origin of humankind have discovered that all 21$^{st}$ century human beings are descendants of a small number of humans who roamed Africa 20,000 years ago. Those predecessors have been tracked genetically to India, China, Australia, the Mid-East, Europe, and over the Bering Strait to the Americas. In this patriarchal society, it is interesting that the tracking was done through maternal genetic markings. In short, all lineage can be traced to African women 20 millennia ago! Everybody!

Then along comes another study. This one tracked human lineage over 2000 generation and was documented in the PBS television film, "Journey of Man." "We are all related," says Dr. Spencer Wells, who contributed to the documentary, "all of the six billion people on earth today. We all can trace our ancestors to 10,000 people who populated Africa 50,000 years or so ago," says Dr. Wells. The study literally traces the journey of men throughout the world by tracking hereditary DNA markers.

Dr. Wells' colleague, Luca Cavalli-Sforza, professor of genetics at Stanford University, reported, "One lesson stands out from all the others about relationships: you, I, in fact, everyone from all over the world — we're all literally African under the skin, brothers and sisters separated by a mere 2000 generations. Old-fashioned concepts of race are not only socially divisive, but scientifically wrong."

or racial background, they are all part of one nation," wrote David Broder, reporter and political analyst for the *Washington Post,* in 1998. He was writing about the need to "remind ourselves of what we have in common and why those values are so precious." His column referred to a survey released by Public Agenda, a nonpartisan public opinion research and education group in New York. That report concluded "that the ties that bind the nation are stronger than some may think." It added, "The real threats to American come not from immigrants but from our taking our freedoms — and our success as a nation — for granted."

## How to Break a Habit

Habits can be broken by a series of three actions. Awareness, Information, and Will:

### *Awareness:*

First it is necessary to become aware of a habit. This book is meant to accomplish that. The world is disintegrating into clusters of Us and Them, aggregates of avowed defenders of "how it's always been," and mobs of frightened owners of habits they are determined to hold onto. This world also contains assemblages of hopeful people working to reduce the conflict by listening to others and vowing to alter both the words and the behavior.

### *Information:*

The second part to breaking a habit is to obtain information — just the facts, and make them *just* facts. Know that the Bible was written in a patriarchal society, that Shakespeare did not portray gay characters. Know that no Latinos signed the Declaration of Independence and that women were left out of the U.S. Constitution. Know that some cultures revere their elders while others dispatch them to the forest or a *home* to die. Know that Indian tribes were the first Americans with a very highly developed culture. Know that constrictions of social intermingling (race, marriage, child bearing, class, and sexual designation) have been created by humans.

***Will:*** The third part of breaking habits is to want to; you need to want to make your world one which treats people fairly and one which regards every person with respect. And this can be accomplished without legislation — without the language police or regulations about how we use words.

We can break habits, the habits established by our forebears. We can learn new ways to embrace those around us — no matter who *They* are.

Life is full of choice. Some have said that life *is* choice. Choose to break the old language habits that exclude others. Choose to correct the image behind your words by using language that translates into an open-minded attitude and by behavior that is courteous, respectful, and fair to all.

# 4

# All Turtles Are
# Not Slow

## Stereotyping
## Euphemisms
## Labels

P eople are speaking faster and faster, and using more
language shortcuts and abbreviations — you know,
those horredous acronyms that can be ambiguous
and subject to misinterpretation.

Blame what you will — the telegraph, telephone,
radio, television, fax, email, Internet, cell phones or electronic gadgets that speak, write and photograph messages.

For whatever reasons, Americans like to speak in a
shorthand that utilizes stereotyping, labels, and euphemisms — anything to spit out words without thinking
about their meanings.

When that happens, the temptation is to make assumptions based on incomplete information. "I have a pet turtle
that moves slowly; therefore, all turtles are slow." Maybe
not! While it is definitely easier to accept the all-things-are
generalization, accuracy often becomes lost.

## Stereotyping

Stereotyping has become a lazy way to identify people
and objects in our world by using the all-things-are thing.
*Stereotype* is defined as "a conventional, formulaic, and

---

## Some of America's History

From the beginning of this country, immigrants to the U.S. huddled together in their ghettos — the Irish, Polish, Germans, Greeks, Russians, Italians, as separated from other groups as blacks were from the mainstream. Neighborhoods formed around religious ideals: Jews, Catholics, Baptists, Methodists, Hindi, Muslim, Shinto .... Most were separated from mainstream America by language — because newcomers often do not speak English.

Until the Civil War, most blacks were confined as slaves to southern plantations. But not all people with dark skin were slaves or came directly from Africa. Many came here from the Caribbean, Central and South America, as well as other parts of the world.

By the end of the 19$^{th}$ century, Americans were defined by their neighborhoods. "Where do you come from?" Not until families began to inter-marry outside their neighborhoods did the Melting Pot concept appear. As immigrants learned English and began to mingle in the workplace, the concept of America, Land of the Free, was developed. By the end of the 20$^{th}$ century, bloodlines had became so intermingled that long, complicated genealogies were needed to untangle most people's heritage.

---

oversimplified conception, opinion, or image." The word describes "a metal printing plate cast from a mold that is used over and over to produce a fixed unvarying form." To stereotype is to lack originality or creativity, resulting in excessive repetition without having to think about it.

Language in the United States arrives from all parts of the world — and with it worldwide bias. The quickest way to deal with this diverse challenge, in America at least, seems to be labels and stereotypes. It's quick and easy! Too easy.

## Age

As the population's median age rises (more people are living longer), the temptation has grown to isolate groups according to age.

*"Those youngsters!"*
*"That old man."*
*"There go the senior citizens."*
*"Oh to be young and foolish again!"*
*"Make way for these old folks."*

Yep! Words as innocuous as these can distinguish a group as outsiders, "not with it, not cool, not our type."

When you are young, you consider the old codgers around you as aliens from a different planet — not at all like you. Somewhere in the 40s or 50s, you may discover you're the filling in the sandwich.

The Sandwich Generation refers to people in the middle, adults taking care of their parents as well as their children. This balancing act is only temporary, thank god, but well defines the quandary of who is old and who is young. When you're in the middle, you belong to both definitions, yet you qualify for discounts in neither. That's the time you look around and discover *you* are becoming *them*.

Meanwhile, perhaps, the only caution is to remember where life is taking you. Likewise, elders need to remember where they've been.

If you are over 30, try picturing a group of kids. What are they doing? Playing or fighting? Are you aware of the large number of youths who are trying to save the earth's environment? If you are under 40, picture a group of retired people. Are they playing shuffleboard or rafting down a whitewater canyon? Were you aware of the many people who retire before the age of 50? This is age stereotyping.

## Gender and Economics

Stereotyping of isms occurs when we slant our questions according to our own perceptions. Here's how sexist role stereotyping works: Close your eyes and picture a doctor, school superintendent, bank president, nurse, teacher and secretary.

Are the first three men and the second three women? That is sexist stereotyping.

Such bias has led to pay discrimination. Historically, women were discouraged from working outside the home until the mid-twentieth century. When women were *allowed* to be the teachers, nurses and secretaries, they accepted low income in order to "serve." As other fields opened to women, they abandoned the low-paying jobs to become administrators, doctors and entrepreneurs. The result is what is apparent in fields of medi-

> ## Discrimination
>
> Discrimination by implication is a matter, not so easily cured by changing endings. Many words have sexist meanings because of long-term stereotyped usage. Because secretaries and nurses historically have been women, the words imply femininity; because attorneys and doctors have been men (fields closed to women for many years), the words imply masculinity. While these discriminating tendencies don't apply anymore, the implications linger on.

cine, education and business today — shortages of committed people who once did the jobs because they wanted to (and were willing to accept low pay). These shortages will continue until pay increases bring committed people back to health care, education and business.

When this bias extends to roles in the workplace, the scope of us all to expand vocational horizons is restricted. Women excel in trade skills that used to be called "nontraditional" jobs for women, and men excel in nurturing skills (still called "women's work").

## Race

Now close your eyes and picture a person of color, a Mexican, an Asian, or an Indian. Are they wearing native costumes? Sombreros, kimonos, saris, feathers? This is cultural stereotyping. In America, you'll find most people with such cultural labels are likely to wear three-piece suits, dresses and uniforms. But wait, perhaps you should have been asked to picture an African-American, Mexican-American, Asian-American or Native-American. Would that change your pictures? This is racial stereotyping.

Two people walk into a convenience store. One has light skin; one has dark skin. One holds up the clerk and runs off with the money. The other calls the police. Who would you guess did what? This is racial bias.

What field of work would you expect a Jewish person to follow? A Chinese? A Mexican? An Arab?

People behave according to their self-perception. Sometimes the perception develops over time according to the way other people see them. When people consider themselves to be clowns, they tend to act like clowns. When males see themselves as tough, powerful men, they carry themselves upright, strong and proud. When they look at themselves as losers, they slump and appear weak. When women perceive themselves as weak, passive and submissive, they stay in the background, apologize for their presence, and meekly accept what is handed them. When women see themselves as winners, they stand tall, speak in direct ways and don't hesitate to voice their opinions.

Americans love to label things, to pigeonhole and name them. Often the first question asked of a pregnant woman is, "Are you having a boy or girl?" The second question usually is, "What are you going to name her (or him)?" When adults talk to children, they ask, "How old are you? What grade are you in? Where do you go to school?" When adults are introduced to other adults, they ask such things as, "Where do you come from? What do you do for a living?" "What's your sign?" We need to know

where to pigeonhole people from the very beginning. We
seldom ask philosophical questions, such as, "How do
you feel about jazz music? What are your favorite books?"
We tend to think that certain roles belong to certain kinds
of people, a certain gender, a certain economic pigeonhole, a certain way of behaving, a certain manner of
appearance. The result becomes circular bias.

## Circular Bias

Circular bias is a familiar way of identifying the world
around us. When we hear certain words, we draw pictures
in our minds automatically, instantly, which reflect our
beliefs about these stereotypes. Then our spoken words
also reflect our own bias. And around it goes.

Do you believe:

*All blacks are poor and on welfare.*
*All Hispanics are illegal aliens.*
*All Asians are conniving, wise, shifty.*
*All mentally ill are dangerous.*
*All disabled people are incapable of....*
*All older people are bumbling incompetents.*
*All children are impatient.*
*All nationalities other than yours are less....*
*All turtles are slow.*

Circular bias results in pigeonholing that is believed by
those so described." If you call me smart, I'll give you
good answers. Or call me apathetic; I don't care!" Labeling
affects the way we behave. If we label our business leaders as business*men*, we are setting up a criterion for
business people to behave as men do. This implies that if
you are a woman, you need to behave as men behave in
order to become a *businessman*.

The labeling of men as *aggressive* and women as
*submissive* may have begun in biology class, where we
were taught that men and women tend to behave in these

ways. What we fail to realize is that all of us are capable of our own choices. Some men have a few *feminine* traits (nurturing relationships, passivity, and submissive behavior); some women have a few of the *masculine* traits (aggression, activity, and powerful behavior). Men tend to display more of the so-called masculine traits, women more of the feminine traits. We now know that both men and women hold potential for a variety of gender differences, but that one gender becomes dominant. We all know men who behave submissively (typically feminine) and women who act aggressively (typically masculine).

Circular bias provides easy, repeatable myths that fill the belief systems that begin with childhood. They include myths of race, age, gender and class. Be aware of the myths used to define people of certain cultures:

"Blacks cannot be educated."

"Asians are sneaky."

"Mexicans can't be trusted."

"Indians are lazy."

Did you ever stop to wonder where those myths originated? Who dreamed them up? Most likely, they originated with white men who feared their jobs were threatened and wanted to keep "those foreigners in their place," just as white men insisted that women were not worthy of being educated (or worse, "didn't want to be educated") and belonged in the home raising children.

Identify the myths of age:

"Children are mischievous troublemakers."

"Old women are dotty."

"Forty-year-old men are restless."

"Children should be seen and not heard."

When are the normal years? Which is the best age?

Here's something else to ponder: Why do we believe that people who are disabled have no "regular" lives, that poor people are losers, and rich folk are successful?

## Reduce the Bias of Stereotyping

Reduce stereotyping with a few simple word tools.

***Omit suffixes:*** Women don't need to have *ette* or *ess* attached to their occupations (waitress, actress, poetess, authoress, majorette, bachelorette). Women can manage very well in an occupation titled *waiter, actor, poet, author, major* and...well, okay, *bachelor* is considered unique to men. (Women aren't meant to be single, and often have to suffer a word such as *spinster.*) We wouldn't think of adding the *ess* or *ette* to journalist, writer, plumber, trucker, executive or computer programmer.

***Control Modifiers:*** Think twice when hauling out the word modifiers: *mischievous, dotty, restless, loser, successful, stupid, greedy, lazy, dishonest, weird,* even *different.* There are those who consider *different* a dirty word; and there are those who relish the label! Avoid using adjectives that restrict or single out race or gender or age or religion.

## Euphemisms

The use of euphemisms is another source of divisive implication in language. "Women's work" falls largely into the low-paying or nonpaying jobs which include clerks, waiters, nurses, teachers, secretaries, tellers and volunteers — the bottom of the economic ladder. Consider the masculine image that accompanies such high-paying professions as lawyer, CEO, doctor, professor, executive, banker, or superintendent.

The use of euphemisms may seem to distract or hide the implied meanings, and are thus used mostly with low-paying jobs. Consider these cover-ups:

Administrative or Executive Assistant (secretary)
Sanitary Engineer (janitor)
Customer Service Representative (clerk/teller)

Domestic Engineer (ugh! homemaker)
Ninety years young... (young?)
Of a certain age (which one?)
Retired (over 65)
Projects resident (black)
Dark-complexioned (person of color)

Euphemisms sometimes are funny; mostly they miss the point.

*Euphemisms* are created to paint over a bias, which is an inclination to exhibit impartial judgment.

A *bias* implies unfairness or a policy stemming from prejudice — pre-judging.

An *ism* moves the bias to another level and encompasses a distinctive theory or doctrine.

Sometimes our actions that become isms display a strong fear of "the other," and are basic to bias. "If they're not like us, something must be wrong — with them."

### Euphemisms

We develop phrases that seem amusing, but point up differences to the degree of silliness: those who wear glasses are "visually challenged;" girls are "pre-women;" short people are "vertically challenged;" tall people are "vertically enhanced;" a housewife is a "domestic engineer;" the unemployed are "vocationally dislocated;" Kermit the Frog is an "Amphibian-American;" the dead are "terminally inconvenienced" or "metabolically different;" and pets are "animal companions." These labels affect people much the same way as hearing a child point to a redhead, an obese person, or anyone who looks different, and remark about what they see.

Euphemisms appear readily for the low-paying or nonpaying jobs, but appear less often for supervisory and professional work. (Why try to create prestige with phony labels?)

## Labels

A label is a short-cut to identification — when identification seems necessary. Remove all the labels from the cans in your cupboard and prove it to yourself. The outsides look alike, but the contents are different.

People too identify only a part of themselves on the outside. Don't make the mistake of comparing external likeness to generalize about the contents. All women (or men) are not...; all people of color (or whites) are not...; all youngsters (or oldsters) are not...;

Accuracy in labeling can be difficult, if not impossible. At one time, the term "minority" was applied to a group of people for legal protection. However, many people object to the term as evoking a feeling of smallness.

> [NOTE: Recall that the term "minority" cannot include women who actually make up a majority of humans.]

When absolutely necessary to identify by skin color or race (and make sure of the necessity), use the preferred label. And keep up to date. Yesterday's "Negroes" are tomorrow's "people of color." Be accurate. Not all "whites" have white skin; not all light-skinned people are "whites." Not all "blacks" have black skin; dark-skinned people come from all corners of the world and in all shades. In the past, the "black and white" terms have been quick-and-easy identifications of ethnic background. (Isn't it interesting that an earlier term, "colored people," has been replaced with "people of color?")

Semantically speaking, all people are "people of color!" So where do we go now?

The switch from identification by skin color to nationality came with an awareness of genealogy (possibly promulgated by the computer). As more people became self-conscious of the term "white," new hyphenated identities were sought: African-American, Polish-American,

Greek-American, German-American, even Cambodian-Irish-Rumanian-American.

Try to connect a color with the national origin: African, Jamaican, Indian (Eastern), Mexican, South American, Australian, English, Russian, Korean, Thai, Cambodian, Vietnamese; middle-European; mid-Eastern …. Get it?

Labels are tricky and often inaccurate. All Arabs are not Palestinians; all middle-European are not Slavic; all Asians are not Chinese (nor are all Chinese from Asia); all English are not white; all Africans are not black. If you find it absolutely necessary to identify according to nationality or culture, ask for the preferred term. More often, you'll realize that you don't really need to know.

Age identification is similar. Sometimes it is important to identify by age. There may be limits of legal or physical importance — but not always. Why, for instance, do newspapers print the age of accident victims? of business people? of actors? of ambassadors? In newspapers, obituaries will find age an important label, but that's about all. Has anyone ever inquired about the age of the City Editor?

You can reduce the isms in your environment and remove them from writing by referring to job categories and professions using accurate terminology, by avoiding the euphemisms that mask an economic deficiency with a fancy title, and by looking closely at the use of labels.

What follows are ways to look at the stereotypical words that people use to *separate*, and some suggestions to close the gap between Us and Them. Find more alternatives in the Glossary at the back of this book.

## BOOMER

The term "baby boomer" was coined to relate to the flood of children that were born following World War II. The expected increase in population was foretold first by the overcrowded grade schools (the 1950s and 1960s), then the colleges (the 1970s and 1980s). The mass of Boomers surged into the job market in the 1980s and 1990s, overloading the system with attorneys, waiters, doctors, business executives, truck drivers, and insurance sales people.

Because the floodgates also let women into these fields, the work force grew in unparalleled leaps; childcare became an issue; traffic lanes became clogged; and jobs became scarce. Now, as predicted, the Boomers face their Social Security years, which results in another overload issue to blame on this Boomer generation.

Use of the term might well be limited to societal issues and not thrown around carelessly to indicate anyone of a certain age.

## CODGER / COOT (POOP) / GEEZER
Ever since Katharine Hepburn lovingly referred to Henry Fonda as "you old poop," in the play "On Golden Pond," the terms "old poop" and "old coot" have taken on new connotations. Old seems to be an unnecessary adjective when used with *coot, fogy* and *codger*.

With people living to more advanced ages, there seem to be more of them around. The terms *fogy, codger* and *coot* speak loudly of incompetence (never mind incontinence), wavering physical and mental strengths, waning ability, diminished power and effectiveness. *Old men, after all, are simply out of it, over the hill, impotent.* Not always true.

Terms such as "old codger," "old coot," or "geezer" are demeaning at best and downright insulting (unless used by Ms. Hepburn or a loving friend). Many of those aging men defended this country in war — to protect rights of free speech, among others. Many of them developed companies that now fulfill your needs for goods and services. Many of them raised decent children who are your neighbors, and perhaps even your relatives. Don't make them regret it!

When dealing with older men, credit them with having years of life and learning stored within those bodies. Sure, they have aged, but while their skin is full of wrinkles and their hair is thinning, their minds are full of experience, just as yours will be in a few (too few) years.

## CRONE

Crones, once considered to be wise aging women, have morphed into the image of wicked stepmother types in current culture. The image is wild hair, staring eyes and inability to speak clearly or remember your name. While these images of old women are out-dated, so is the image of "grandma" as a lovely white-haired old lady. Grandma doesn't knit mittens and bake cookies as she once did. Now Grandma cruises the Bahamas, practices yoga on Tuesdays and Thursdays, drives a sports car, and operates her own business.

Anthropologists once looked for a reason that human women lived beyond their childbearing years when females of other species do not. Now comes information about a tribe in Northern Tanzania where post-menopausal women are the serious breadwinners. Contrary to the paradigm of father-hunts-and-mother-raises-the-young, it appears that these older women work long hard hours in the bush to provide food for the table. In our own culture, grandmothers often care for older children while the mother cares for infants or holds down a job outside the home. And many of these mothers are in that over-50 category that buttons down the idea that senior women, indeed, are an important part of the clan.

Another image is missing. That is because many older women are invisible. In a mixed crowd, young people receive attention, old people are passed up. In advertising, models are young, targeting a market from ages 18 to 45, unless the product is in need of a "crazy old mother-in-law." Talk about stereotypes!

See older women as acquiring years of life and learning, women whose bodies age as their minds fill with experience. Women over the childbearing years have learned to use their time to care for themselves and others, and to share themselves with their communities through both volunteer and profit-making work.

There's a restaurant on the West Coast that this author will never again enter because of a server who insisted on addressing me as "sweetie" and (ugh!) "sweet pea." I was in the city to read from my books on nonsexist language.

A note to young people dealing with older people. Try not to use baby talk and a baby tone of voice with them. Don't treat oldsters as "cute" or "sweet" or "darling" or (god forbid) "sweet pea" — children that need to be explained to. Your respect and awe are the best gifts you can give seniors — they've earned both. An ironic piece of modern culture is that with one hand we applaud elders who continue to exercise their work ethic and with the other we fire 55-year-olds because they are too old.

## GAY / QUEER / LESBIAN

Consider the number of words that have been applied to people who are (or who are considered to be) homosexual. The truth of homosexuality may one day become accepted as sexual orientation, accepted in that the stigma of homosexuality will be removed. In the meantime, words that demean a person's sexual preference can be avoided. The terms *homosexual, bi-sexual, transvestite* or *transsexual* have specific meanings that are best not to be confused with *gay, queer,* or even *lesbian*. Preferred terms for homosexual men and women are *gay* and *lesbian*.

Consider the term "straight," which suggests "acceptable," with anyone else as "crooked" or "contorted." Once again, the words for *Us* suggest "the norm," and *They* are the "irregular, the outsiders, the come-latelys, the alsos." Really now, how often is a person's sexual preference anyone else's business?

## GIRL / GAL — BOY / MAN

According to biological definition, a girl is a feminine human who has not reached puberty. *Gal* is just another way to say *girl*. (Actually, it is a British pronunciation of "girl.") Both terms apply to females up to the age of mid- or late-teens. Generally, girls become young women about the age of 14. Both *girl* and *gal* are demeaning when applied to adult women, whether

> **How to insult a man:**
>
> Think for a moment of all the words used to demean women, words that refer to women and girls as animals (cow, hen, chick), or as objects (honey, sugar, dish), or worse. Now try to think of words to demean men. You'll come up with a few words meaning "stupid or oafish," even "bastard" or "brute." But the worst things you can call a man are "sissy," "woman" or "girl."

or not it is thought "cute" to refer to older women as such. (Notice that models, prostitutes, entertainers, and women in service jobs tend to be referred to as *girls?*)

Likewise, a boy is a masculine human who has not reached puberty. Consider how demeaning is the term boy when referring to a man.

If both sexes of people of similar age are referred to as girls and boys, the terms are acceptable. The discrimination occurs when boys of a particular age are referred to as *men*, while the girls are still called *girls*.

Example:

The following teams are made up of young people under the age of 14. Yet, we read: "The men's basketball team won by 6 points; the girls' team won by 17."

As for the term "guys and gals," let's leave that to current jargon and hope it goes away. The term seems to be used to avoid "men and women," removing the equality in a very subversive way. Even more insulting is the use of *guys* to include everyone. The next time a waiter or clerk asks, "How are you guys today?" when talking a group of women, especially older women, you should expect mayhem in the place.

It's okay to discriminate age-wise with the use of the word *girl*. Just be sure to save it for females under the age of 14. Address adult women as *women*, not *girls* or *gals,* and certainly not *guys*.

## HYPHENATED AMERICANS

People who hold citizenship in the United States are considered Americans. But hold on there! Aren't people from South America also Americans? Or from Guatamala? Or Mexico? Or Canada?

Citizens of the United States are so ethnocentric as to believe that only Americans live in the States and all who live in the States are Americans. What's more, Americans feel there is something to be proven by adding the term to another heritage.

If you're faced with using *African-American*, do you equally use *Italian-American* or *Swedish-American*? These references apply only to nationality, not race. All Africans are not dark-skinned. All dark Americans are not African. Africa is a continent of nations, not a skin color!

Do you use *Chinese-American* or *Asian-American* with people who have never been farther west than California?

To be absolutely accurate, it would be necessary to indicate the entire family history: *Sioux-Irish-German-Italian-Arabian-Syrian-Mesopotamian-American*. And that can become very complicated.

If it is necessary to designate heritage according to a birth country, or the birth countries of ancestors, go ahead. But if that is not necessary, skip it! In too many cases, the genealogical background of Americans becomes too complicated and too easy to generalize.

## LADY

The term *lady* is difficult to define because of many current usage connotations. In most cases, the word evokes standards of propriety and elegance, such as in *first lady* and *leading lady*. In others, a definition of *lady* refers to her behavior, as with a *lady of the evening* or *lady in waiting*. *Lady* has been defined as "slangy, pompous, presumptuous, and patronizing," depending on the tone of voice.

Other times, the word indicates diminution, as in *cleaning lady, saleslady,* and *forelady*. These are condescending subterms for *clean-up man, salesman,* and *foreman*, and imply that women are doing men's jobs. Thus the terms are uncomplimentary. Use instead terms that accurately define the work: *janitor, sales representative/agent,* and *supervisor*.

The jury is still out as to the meaning of the possessive *my lady*, when referring to a female friend. Even when it is said with stars in the man's eyes, the term has undertones of possessiveness in it.

Watch how some men use the word *lady* to avoid using the more acceptable *woman*. Listen to the way some men even hesitate before using either word. Is that reverence? or fear?

A sub-meaning for the use of *lady* is the use of the gratuitous adjective before a noun, as in *lady doctor,* or *lady's tool kit*. What's wrong with simply *doctor* or *tool kit*? Another term with sub-meaning is *lady of the house*. This becomes a patronizing term to encourage the woman to feel important and propel her into a mood to buy something. Put-downs occur when *lady* is used to identify the gender of a person behind the job title or other label. When tempted to use *lady attorney, lady pharmacist,* or *lady driver,* forget the gender-referenced adjective and stick with just the noun — *attorney, pharmacist, driver.* Unless, of course, you would equally refer to *guy* attorney, *gentleman* pharmacist, or *man* doctor.

Example:
S: *The lady lawyer and the young attorney had lunch.*
N: *The two lawyers had lunch.*

S: *Surgery was performed by the lady resident doctor.*
N: *Surgery was performed by the resident doctor.*

While you're avoiding *lady doctor,* keep away from *male nurse, male secretary,* and *male teacher.* Sexism in language occurs with both sexes.

If identification by gender is really necessary, once is enough in a news article or report. Use the words *woman* or *man,* as in *woman prime minister, woman judge, man secretary,* or *man agent.* Even then, make the distinction only if it is pertinent.

## MANHOOD / WOMANHOOD

The state of being a man or a woman is referred to as *manhood* or *womanhood.* While the word structure is similar, the connotations are not.

Perhaps the clearest indication of the difference is found in the negative reference, "a threat to his manhood," compared to "a threat to her womanhood." Somehow, men consider their threat more serious than women's.

Visualize a man in a skirt. What this does to threaten his manhood can be seen in the reactions of other men.

Most are aghast that a man would think so little of his manhood that he would don women's clothing (unless perhaps you are the Prince of Wales wearing the royal kilts or a Greek guard wearing the traditional foustanella).

Now visualize a woman in trousers. This doesn't seem to threaten a woman's womanhood — at least not in the same way. Most women don slacks and no one has thought much about it since 1938 when Marlene Dietrich first appeared in public wearing them. So why is cross-dressing so demeaning to men and of little concern to women?

Whatever the reason, there are words that do the same damage to manhood as wearing a skirt. These are the words that question the virility of a man, that question his "really being a man." And those words begin with *sissy* in childhood and grow into *effeminate, lightweight,* or *like a girl* in adulthood. These are fighting words, literally, to many men, words deserving of physical defense of one's manhood.

Conversely, women don't cringe in the same way at being referred to as masculine. In some instances, it is meant as a compliment. ("She performed as well as a man," may seem like a compliment to some, but disguises a patronizing insult.) Words that describe or insinuate a woman's sexual preference don't seem to bring out the deep-seated anger in women that they bring out in men.

In an episode of the television sitcom, "The Bill Cosby Show," Dr. Huxtable surveys a plumbing repair job and comments to the plumber (a woman), "That looks like a two-man job." To which she replies, "It could be a two-man job or it could be a one-woman job." Whose *–hood* was more wounded, hers at being patronized as not being able to conduct her work efficiently or his at being told one woman could handle the job that otherwise might require two men?

Of course, comedy uses these terms for effect. And much humor is based on the sarcasm or mockery of social mores. But humor aside, consider the effect of words that question sexual identity. It seems clear that comedy reflects serious concerns; which may explain why so many TV sit-coms deal with sexual identity and gender roles?

## STEP-MOTHER / MOTHER-IN-LAW

Oh the jokes! And the put-downs for in-laws and step-relatives. And they usually demean the women involved. There aren't many jokes about wicked stepfathers or overbearing fathers-in-law.

A family is made up of parents and children and grandparents and aunts and uncles and cousins ... and new spouses of divorced parents ... and their children ... and relatives of the spouses that marry into the family ... and their children ... and on and on. Exercise the use of "my family," as opposed to my *step-son, sister-in-law,* or their *step-mom* (unless that specificity is required).

And isn't it wonderful how large and complex a family can become? All the more reason to honor everyone who could possibly be called part of your family.

## SWARTHY / WHITEY

Any term to draw attention to the color of a person's skin is discrimination of the highest order. Just how dark is *swarthy?* And what about someone with "olive skin?" To many people, that might indicate green. Could you describe a person who has spent time in a tanning parlor as *swarthy* or *olive-skinned?* Of course. But would it matter?

Avoid terms that indicate skin color, unless discussing skin color or race issues. When tempted to use colors, black, brown, swarthy, olive, dark-complexioned, white, red-skinned, yellow, green, give it up. Trying to trace heritage through skin color has become as difficult as trying to trace through genetic background and nationality.

The next time you're in a crowded room, scan the faces of the people there and try to attach a specific color to each one. The first thing you notice is that there is not a single white face in the room. The second thing is there is not likely to be a single black face. There are, however, various shades of tan, beige, peach, reddish (an affliction having to do with "white" faces), ecru, brown, dark brown.... And again, does it matter? What color, exactly, is your face?

## TEENYBOPPERS

It is unclear if young people have ever been asked how they feel about this term: *teenybopper*. Ask the teenagers in our life and find out. But please, do not regard them as "green" or "still wet behind the ears." There are many teenagers out there applying to prestigious schools, carrying 3.5-plus grade averages, holding down responsible jobs, caring for their siblings, concerned about the environment, and spending time in community activities. Get to know them — and remember how adults spoke and behaved toward you when you were a *teenybopper*!

## TOMBOY / SISSY

Children begin to receive word messages about their sexual identities long before they know what "sexual identity" means. Use of words like *tomboy* or *sissy* to youngsters confuses their self-perception and sense of sexual identity (whether they know the words or not). Children have a rough enough time learning who they are without having to overcome such words used in derision.

When referring to a girl who is active, use words like *strong, vigorous, adventuresome, spirited, competitive*, and *self-confident*. But avoid the use of *tomboy*.

When referring to a boy who is sensitive, use words like *quiet, perceptive, understanding, caring, artistic, introspective, gentle, modest* and *peaceful*. But don't use *sissy*. Be aware that the word *sissy* denotes a put-down, even when applied to a girl.

## WIFE / HUSBAND

A *wife* is a woman married to a man. A *husband* is a man married to a woman. One does not own or supersede the other. It is inaccurate to use "man and wife." Rather, use "husband and wife" or "woman and man." There is no prescribed order, either word could be first.

When two people marry, one does not become the property of the other; one does not belong to the other. Likewise, two married people do not become one, implying two half-people. Two married people become two people sharing their lives.

Certain words used to indicate the spouse can imply "an appendage or chattel." Avoid using degrading terms as *the wife, the little woman, my wife, my better half, the ball and chain, trophy wife, just a wife, my husband, my jailer, my old man,* or *my meal ticket.*

And watch out for implications of "tagging along" with a spouse, such as *faculty wife, corporate wife, senate wife,* and *neighbor's wife.* A recent news story about a judge insisted on referring to her husband by name and to her as "his wife." Professional women have names, just like their husbands. (The professor, senator, or doctor may object to the reference of her spouse as a wife!)

Unless … and now we come to terminology for gay and lesbian married partners. Again, as with any doubt about respectful terminology, ask for preferences. Most gay and lesbian couples appreciate the courtesy. Unless otherwise informed, use genderless terminology: spouse, partner, or companion.

## WOMEN AS ENTITIES

Define women by who they are, not by their fathers or husbands, nor by their children or grandchildren. Women do things besides marry and have children, and they need to be recognized for all of their accomplishments.

Whether or not a woman prefers to use *Mrs., Miss,* or *Ms.*, use her first name only as often as men use their first names. Too often women address men as "Mr. So-and-So," while men address women by their first names. Notice how often women address professional men as "Mr." or "Dr." while hearing themselves addressed as "Betty," "Ann," or even worse, "sweetheart" or "dear"!

When writing to or talking to women, don't use "Mrs. Ben Adams." She would be better referred to with her own name, "Betty Adams," "Mrs. Betty Adams," or "Ms. Betty Adams." To decide which to use, learn her preference. Ask her. You may also ask yourself if this reference would be appropriate if used for a man. Mr. Ben Adams most likely would not stand still for being called "Mr. Betty Adams." If you don't know a woman's preferred title, use a respectful one, as you would in addressing a man that you didn't know well.

Many older people object to dropping the titles they consider respectful — Mr., Mrs. or Ms. — claiming that society is losing its dignity. If you sense that is the case, use the respectful title. Better yet, ask the individual what usage they prefer.

Regarding the reference to one's children (or other household associations), ask yourself whether it would make sense to use the reference to children with the opposite sex. A woman is more than a "housewife," "grandmother," or "mother of three."

In a news item, is the subject identified by the role played in the news story (victim, accused, suspect) or is the subject identified by personal roles and descriptions?

Examples::

> *The juror is a mother of three children* (only if another juror is identified as *the father of two*). The family status may be important to the story; usually it is not.

> Margaret Thompson has been a member of the Board of Directors for six years. *She is the wife (mother or grandmother) of....* (Only if you similarly would say: Marvin Thompson has been a member of the Board of Directors for six years. *He is the husband (father or grandfather) of....*

## WOMEN AS THINGS

American English offers perfectly good pronouns to identify people, using gender terms: *she, he, her, him*. Inanimate things are identified with the pronoun *it*. Save gender words for people, and then only if they apply.

A man is properly referred to with masculine pronouns and possessive adjectives: *he him*, and *his*. A woman is properly referred to by feminine pronouns and possessive adjectives: *she, her*, and *hers*.

Personification of boats, autos, hurricanes, machines, and so on, as sexual beings is both incongruent and inaccurate. Avoid such terms as "give her the gas," or "she's a real twister this time!" or "the mechanic should have her ready in a half-hour."

Conversely, avoid using terms of things for people. Avoid referring to a woman as *cookie, sugar, honey, a dish, a tomato, a doll, a clinging vine, a wallflower*, or *a fashion plate*. Do you realize that nuclear power plants are referred to as "sister plants," or that elements of radioactive decay are referred to as "element's daughters"? And that hardware items often have "male and female parts"? These terms are particularly demeaning to women in the light of women's efforts toward peacemaking.

## DON'T *Dear* ME!

Just a few words about *dear*. When someone calls a woman to whom they are not closely related "dear," the term is insulting. Some men (especially older ones) enjoy using this term with women, justifying it by calling the term "friendly." However, these men would be unlikely to use *dear* with other men to be "friendly," and that is what makes it discriminatory and demeaning.

Women who use similar terms with men they don't know (or hardly know) are using the same demeaning process. Some think that a woman clerk or waiter who uses terms like "honey" or "dear" is attempting to position herself on a more equal footing with the man she is waiting on.

This idea points strongly to the method of using *endearing* terms with strangers as a way of exhibiting power — male or female. A woman calling another woman "dear" is likely seeking the same thing.

Likewise, a stranger who addresses an older woman as "dear" is demonstrating the most outrageous act of patronizing language and risks a violent reaction that may or may not stop with a swat alongside the head.

## X- AND Y-GENERATIONS

The X-generation are the children of Boomers. They make up the major work force. The X-ers blossomed with the '90s technology boom, and they swam with the fishes until the bust of the 21$^{st}$ century economy. They are the ones now starting over, borrowing money, floundering in the job market, and learning to do without.

The X-ers' children, the Y-generation, still haven't learned about the effect of world economy on their lives. Overcrowding, terrorism, and dwindling resources may be their teachers. As yet, no one has dared to consider the Z-generation.

## Inclusive Do's and Don'ts

1] Stay away from terms and phrases that tend to diminish or demean other persons because of their skin color, their genes, their gender or age or...hey, why not just stay away from terms that demean or diminish?

2] There are some general terms you may not have even thought about: *greatest woman golfer of the club! darn good for a woman! a man who can cook? and he's gentle too!* Acknowledge a good golf game as a personal achievement, just as you would a person's abilities, whether man or woman.

3] Vary the order of placement. Words can imply second-class or second place. Vary familiar terms, such as *husband and wife, man and woman, his and hers,* or *fathers and mothers.* Avoid the subliminal message of men first, women second.

You can change stereotypes by using: *wife and husband, woman and man, hers and his,* and *mothers and fathers.*

Observe the parallel treatment of terms:
Women and men (adults)
Boys and girls (children)

4] Parenthetical inclusion of women also is insulting. Rewrite if necessary, but avoid the afterthought implication found in such terminology as:

S: *All company men (and women) are invited.*
*The instructions apply to boys (and girls) under 10.*

N: *All company women and men are invited.*
*The instructions apply to boys and girls under 10.*

or:
*All company employees are invited.*
*The instructions apply to all children under 10.*

5] Learn to regard differences as positive and natural parts of being human. If you're young, take time to appreciate those who are older (gasp!) and learn from them. If you are old, take a good look at those youngsters and appreciate their energy. That once was you.

If your skin is one color, would you want all of humanity to have the same tone? Come on now, light skin burns easily and needs a lot of care to keep from turning uncomfortable in sunlight. Dark skin has its problems too, feeling rough and scaly, and difficult to keep soft. Brown skin is neither light nor dark; is that the ideal? And whose skin is actually red (other than those with vein problems or high blood pressure)? Do Asians actually have yellow skin?

Consider how terms referring to women are used, and give thought to how similar terms are used when referring to men. All women are created equal (and men too)!

Don't you hate the driver's license that insists you choose a hair color? Make a list of the attributes that define your own appearance. Are the traits that define you all positive? Has anyone ever used one of those attributes to put you down? Grey hair, kinky hair, baldness, acne, crossed eyes, skin color, nose shape, ear size, one-eyebrow, slanted eyes, weight, or the inability to walk, hear or see? How did that feel?

Take another look at that turtle — that slow, cumbersome, awkward animal — on land. Now take a look at it in the water. Do you see how fast it swims? Faster than many of the fish that try to keep up! Don't assume that "all turtles are slow." And don't assume that "all people of a certain description are…!"

Words can be hurtful or healing. Take care with the words you choose.

# 5

# I Hate Me!

## The Damage of Hate Words
## Verbal Abuse
## Healing Words

Behavior begins with words. If the words become hateful, the behavior is hateful. If the words are loving, the behavior is loving.

We hate what we don't understand and therefore fear.

We hate those we feel have more (or less) than we do.

We hate those who we suspect are better than us.

We hate people who aren't like us.

Hate words have grown into hate crimes in the United States and around the world. The hate begins with scrawled words and whispered mutterings that vilify others, then words that are spoken aloud, followed by words shouted in anger. As a fueled fire rages out of control, the hate words burst into the flames of outright violence.

Strangely, the causes for the differences that fuel the fires are disappearing. Take racism, for instance.

The *We* and *They* are becoming more difficult to identify from external characteristics. Distinct racial categories are being blurred by intermarriage and time. The major "Theys" in America once were the British and French colonists who broke into America in the 17th century and began to push back the natives. At about the same time, American colonists divided themselves between Tories (loyal to England) and Independents (that raucous bunch of boisterous upstarts that included George Washington, Benjamin Franklin, Thomas Jefferson and John Adams). They were followed by the Polish, Germans and middle European immigrants of the 1800s. Then came the Irish and the Italians and the Russians. The recent influx of Asians from Vietnam, Cambodia, and Korea adds to vast numbers of Chinese and Japanese who came to this country a hundred years ago. Now Pacific Islanders and Hispanics (from Mexico, Cuba, Puerto Rico) and middle Easterners (from India, Egypt, the Arab countries) are joining the ranks of Americans. Where once blacks were the main target of villification, now people of any color draw the attention of hatemongers.

No other nation in the world is comprised of people from every other country on this earth. That in itself is mind-boggling. But wait, there's more. The United States is leading the world as a powerful, intelligent, and economically sound nation. Must be we're doing something right.

With the "foreigner" or "they" becoming difficult to define, you'd think the haters would give up. The latest census underscored the difficulty and met the challenge by adding still another line to the ethnic identity check-off: *Multiracial*. What do you want to bet that by the next census, the ethnic identity will be missing? (Wild cheering!)

Who will we call *They* as racial differences become more blurred? In California, no single ethnic or racial group currently makes up a majority. Once we believed the "majority" was comprised of white Christian men. While they have claimed a majority in the United States, they are definitely minorities in the global picture, and are rapidly becoming minorities in this country too. Men biologically are outnumbered by women. Whites are becoming less distinguishable in America, and Christianity is taking a backseat to Judaism and Islam.

The implication in *We and They* is called *otherness* and pops up in all the isms. As racial diversity diminishes, identification issues have been shifted in a variety of other directions — class, body traits, sexual preference, age, and politics (witness the fury of the 2004 national elections).

Nit-picking? Perhaps. Still, it seems human to feel "different" from others — whether superior or inferior — which results in seeking someone to hate. Check with your psychologist as to the origins of hate, but it usually results in finding someone who is "other" to beat up on.

To avoid isms of all kinds, pay attention to the way pronouns are used. If you are under thirty, *We* might translate as *young* and *They* might translate as *old*. If you're over forty, it could be the other way around: *We* are old and *They* are young.

Other pairs to watch out for:

we (the rich)      they (the poor)
we (the poor)      they (the rich)
we (the skinny)  they (the fat)
we (the fat)        they (the skinny)
we (the black)    they (the white)
we (the white)    they (the black)
we (the ins)       they (the outs)
we (the outs)      they (the ins)
we (the normal)  they (the oddities)
we (the familiar) they (the different)
or the other way around.

## Hate Begins With Words

Words can be used either as weapons or as healers, depending on the choice and the manner in which they are spoken. Words can be as sharp and detrimental as swords.

And whether or not they result in physical violence, they still hurt.

Even such unobtrusive words as *mother* and *baby* can hurt others if spoken with a demeaning tone of voice.

Verbal jabs of "cry baby," "mother's boy," and "your mother!" often are used with the intent to hurt. Children particularly are good at this. Watch a playground for a few minutes and you'll see kids using words to hurt others (probably because they know that physical attacks would threaten their own wellbeing).

At the turn of the 21st century, a report on words and children indicates that teasing of children by peers, teachers or parents has a lasting effect on them. It also suggests that teasing words may contribute to the violence of children on playgrounds and in schools. And we thought that "Sticks and stones would never hurt."

One of the big problems in schools is bullying. This is not a new phenomenon, just a new awareness of a very old problem. School bullies have been around probably as long as schools have been around.

School bullies come in all sizes and shapes and levels of economy. It was once thought that bullies were big fellows who came from poverty-stricken families — underprivileged, overgrown, unpopular boys who needed to beat up on younger or smaller kids to get their jollies.

Wrong! On several counts. Ask any teacher — or student. Bullies can be large or small, rich or poor, boys or girls. And know that teasing is nothing less than bullying with a smile. "Making fun of" someone is cruel.

Those spunky, angry, little boys or girls can (and do) attack the overgrown (insecure) kids; and the big girls or boys continue to pick on the little ones. The rich attack the poor who may dress differently or carry sack lunches or wear strange shoes; the poor attack the rich kids with snazzy clothes and lunch money.

Some elementary schools have instituted a novel program of self-governing to deal with the bully problem. The program is called "conflict management" and trains students to monitor the playground and hallways. When disputes arise, the Conflict Managers follow a specific pattern for helping their peers talk out problems and reach workable solutions.

Gee whiz! If children can use words to deal with bullies who threaten others, certainly adults should be able to figure out similar solutions!

Words can be used without the direct threat of bodily harm, and are often the weapons of choice for bullies. Unfortunately bullying doesn't always stop with words.

## Words Escalate

Increased to great intensity, hate-filled and negative words can induce physical reaction in the victim — feeling sick or becoming careless. As soon as a playground bully senses their words have taken effect, the level of animosity rises, and results in physical action.

Adults carry out a kind of verbal abuse by sneering at little boys who act like *girls,* or little girls who act like *boys.* Somehow, the words come out to mean something worse for the girlish little boys than for the boyish little girls. If these words are powerful when slung by children, think how much more powerful they become when the words come from adults — parents, relatives or teachers.

Verbal abuse festers into physical abuse if given time. The escalation from verbal to physical abuse is an insidious long-term process of devaluation. With children, the words are often accompanied with jabs, bumps or kicks. When attacked physically over time, a child will finally have enough and fight back, either with a reactive punch or kick. At this juncture, the war is on and will probably end up in the principal's office.

With adults, it begins the same way with such seemingly harmless terms as *girl, girlie, just-like-a-woman, the little woman, mama's boy, sissy, boy, kid, golden ager, colored, Afro, senior citizen, codger, kids,* and *them.* The victim who acknowledges the nasty tone of voice and the demeaning words, sooner or later, will fight back.

Repetition over time exacts its toll. With adults, there is no principal's office; there is a prison cell, a hospital bed or a coroner's office.

And it all starts with words. We often hear a battered woman confess that her batterer had been calling her names, scolding, and referring to her as his "possession" for years before the physical battering took place?

Black leaders in the 1970s, in an effort to encourage self-esteem in black children, sought to counteract much of the verbal indignity heaped on them by generations of whites who couldn't see past skin color. Their message was what all children need to hear: *I am worthwhile. I am valuable. I am important. I am me!* The results were evident in a generation of black children who gloried in being black. "Black is beautiful," came alive.

Abuse occurs between the powerful and the weak, whether men or women, one race or another, one age group or another, the educated or ill-educated, rich or poor, or between the physically strong or the physically weak.

Toni Morrison, awarded the Nobel prize in literature, told her audience in her acceptance speech, "Oppressive language does more than represent violence; it *is* violence; does more than represent the limits of knowledge; it limits knowledge ... it must be rejected, altered and exposed."

Definite links are being uncovered to the relationship between verbal and physical abuse. We're learning that the strong who verbally abuse are just biding time until they escalate to physical abuse (if no intervention or help occurs along the way). Why not! When words are used by men to demean women, when one race insults another, when adults talk down to children or children snap at elders, the images in the listeners' heads are of worthlessness, of being less than ..., of having no power.

Women who are verbally abused consider themselves as objects, things, possessions, because that's what (powerful) men are telling them. When men refer to women as objects, they are calling them *less than,* and they are battering them as much as if they were hitting them physically.

Likewise, when women regard men as the source of their troubles, the weak little boys who require strong mothering, they may behave in ways that reflect their beliefs, hence, the *hen-pecked husband.* Interestingly, women who belittle men don't refer to them as things, but as weak or feminine-like. Verbal abuse assumes many forms, but is consistently hurtful.

## Words of Warning

Words of verbal abuse that warn of more to come have been identified in a number of ways:

- Phrases that make others responsible for your feelings ("You make me angry," or "You're hurting me by not doing what I tell you.")
- Claiming hurt feelings when really angry ("You hurt my feelings when you told me no" or "You hurt my feelings by turning away.")
- Ranting about injustices of that which is a part of life ("Why can't the government make laws about that?" or "Women shouldn't be allowed to smoke in public.")
- Blaming the person who has been battered ("You made me do it!")
- Threatening violence ("If you do that again, I'll break your neck.")

- Constant criticizing, saying hurtful things, using degrading curses, ugly names or derogatory nicknames.

If there were a cure for this malaise of society, we would be showering the discoverer of it with riches and fame. However, people being humans, men will continue to abuse women verbally (most likely to shore up their own failing sense of importance) and women will continue to treat men in kind (to give themselves a sense of superiority). Just as likely, one race will push against another, the young will downgrade the old, and the old will scoff at the young. The strong will continue to take advantage of the weak.

The importance of this knowledge is that when we feel secure about ourselves, we don't have to inflict our feelings of inferiority upon others. We don't have to attempt to increase our own feelings of importance or more power by knocking down others. We don't have to compile our power highs by making others feel weak and worthless.

Verbal abuse occurs whenever someone feels left out or insecure. People with low self-esteem use words to bolster their feelings. They pick on people who are different, or who are *Them*.

Whether children or adults, verbal abusers undergo the same feelings and face the same results. Words of hatred lead to physical violence. And all because the ones spreading the hatred feel insecure with themselves.

## Who Really Hurts?

Those who are most diminished by bullying or verbal assault, surprisingly, are the abusers themselves, the ones who use the hate words. Any good therapist will tell you that people who spew hatred at others are doing so because they hate themselves.

Perhaps that children's ditty about sticks and stones should be sung with emphasis on different words: Sticks and stones can break my bones, but names will never hurt...*me!* (But it could hurt *you!*)

The extremists — on both ends of a spectrum — are quick to shower hateful words on those whom they choose as targets. Both hate-filled skinheads and sharp-tongued "prayer groups" are equally skilled with using words that cut deeply into foes.

When religious zealots scream about love at the top of their voices, the result is similar to the zealous shouts of those claiming racial purity.

When racists swagger and scowl and spit out their venom, you can be sure that their insides are churning inside the intensity of their own hatred — hatred of themselves and hatred for what they are doing. Likewise, religious zealots harbor a similar strong hatred for their own inadequacies.

What haters are doing reflects what has been done to them. By spewing hate at someone else, they believe they will feel better about themselves. It doesn't work that way.

Hateful words intensify the hateful feelings, and can easily escalate into hateful behavior. To protect themselves, many of the haters seek out other haters to give substance to their own hate. Hate groups become strong temporarily, but eventually burn themselves out. Somewhere along the line, understanding arrives to explain why delivering hatred through words somehow only adds to the hate that the speaker feels.

The danger comes when hate drives people from using words toward using actions to hurt others or themselves. The results are found in prisons, institutions, and morgues.

It all begins with words.

## Healing Words

While we readily acknowledge the killing power of malicious words, we are slow to acknowledge the healing power of words, the value of words to motivate and strengthen, the ability of words to soothe and calm.

The solution is so simple: treat others as you want to be treated. Is that golden, or what?

Learn about what you don't know; ask questions; Read. Accept who you are, and accept others for who they are. Appreciate what others have to offer — and appreciate their differences.

Much of this book looks at the words that hurt or demean. As a respite, let's look at some very powerful words that can actually make people feel better.

Do you remember having a parent kiss the hurt? Whether it was the effect of the kiss or the loving words that accompanied the ministrations, you somehow felt better immediately. Sprinkle your vocabulary with some of the following words and notice how much calmer you feel and how much happier others around you feel.

*Pleasant — Smile — Love — Adore — Pretty — Lovely — Sweet — Calm — Soft — Gentle — Slow — Hug — Strong — Capable — Intelligent — Wise — Smart*

Memorize these words and the following phrases and distribute them liberally throughout your day.

It's okay.

Let me help.

You have a gracious manner.

There, there, things will get better.

Your eyes are sparkling today.

Good job!

Don't worry — I've done the same thing.

Do you need help?

You are so talented at what you do.

Let me hold the door for you.

I hear what you're telling me and I understand.

How do you want to be called?

You are special.

*I love you.*

# 6

# Tell Me Again I'm No Good!

## Words That Diminish and Demean

**W**ords can be hurtful without being spewed out in venomous derision. To illustrate how subversive words work, condider the sarcastic remark to a woman: "I like your dress; I always have!" Or the snide comment, "Well, you look nice today. What have you done with yourself?"

Diminishing words like the above can be carefully calculated to hurt, or can be spoken innocently, often in haste. Still, they retain the power to damage.

### A Test of Language Myths...

1) What is the difference between a chef and a cook?

2) What is the difference between a Boomer and an X-er?

3) How old is a codger? a crone?

4) How dark is swarthy?

5) How does a Y-generation teenybopper behave?

6) How come African-Americans are poor?

7) Teasing doesn't hurt children.

## The Myths

The following comments are simple if you accept the words in the context of current usage. Look closely at the myths, the labels, and the implications.

1) *Chefs are revered, usually men, highly paid; cooks are paid very little and usually are women.* (Okay, go look in the kitchens of five of your friends.)

2) *Boomers are over-the-hill, nearing old age and X-ers are bouncing into their most productive years. Y-ers are still wet behind the ears.* This tongue-in-cheek answer may vary depending on your age.

3) *A codger is really over-the-hill, barely able to make coherent sounds, generally male, and unable to understand very much. The crone? She's a wicked old woman who eats X-ers for breakfast.* Again, this response depends upon your age.

4) *A person with swarthy looks has mixed blood. Swarthy* is an old term that once implied mixed race. In the 21$^{st}$ century, as *races* become more and more mixed, the term is becoming outdated. Other terms, such as *mulatto, half-breed, mongrel, quadroon,* even *miscegenation,* have lost their punch as derisive words. All humans at this point of evolution can consider themselves of "mixed blood," hybrid — homogenized. Anyone walking the earth today is likely to carry genes from a variety of racial backgrounds. Simple DNA chemistry is making this apparent.

5) *Teenyboppers of the Y-generation are senseless, headstrong, mindless, lazy, aimless children who think about nothing that isn't electronic, glitzy, fast and costs a lot.* Once more, how old are you?

6) *Blacks have grown up in ghettos and therefore can't afford education or nice clothes.* This myth is so outworn, it borders on ridiculous. Tear these beliefs apart and look closely: *people of color* come in many shades and nationalities and cannot be lumped in general categories; ghettos usually are formed by cultural similarities, not necessarily economic levels.

7) *Teasing damages some children for the rest of their lives. Young minds accept what is given them, particularly words of grownups.* You don't believe that? Remember your own childhood! Did a parent, teacher, an aunt or uncle tell you that you'd grow up to be a worthless failure, a slut, a lady-killer? a singer, dancer, writer, doctor, judge, mechanic, architect ...? Did someone tell you how beautiful you are? how strong? how funny? how weird? Did you believe them and did those words affect your choices as a grownup?

Occasionally it becomes necessary to stand up and announce a different way of thinking. When we replace "colored" with "Afro-American," then "African-American," then "black," are we simply replacing one word with another? The meaning remains the same: a person whose skin is a certain shade of brown (even though no one can state just which shade that is) and who is often discriminated against because of the darkness of that skin. We're not changing how people think, just how we talk — which can be meaningless.

Words that cannot be used equally with both male and female humans, with all ages, with all cultural backgrounds and nationalities are considered to be discriminatory. The real test is: can *this* term be used for the "other"?

## Words That Diminish and Demean
Many words in the American language imply gender, race, religion or age, either through endings or through general

cultural usage. What mind-pictures appear when encoun-
tering words such as *teacher, professor, consultant, nurse,
janitor, doctor, secretary, computer nerd, taxi driver*, or
*boss*? Many words loudly *imply* gender, race, and age
when they need not. These words themselves sound
inoffensive (okay, maybe not *nerd*); the problem lies in
the interpretation of those words that evoke gender / race
/ age-specific images. When we use one word and expect
listeners to hear the inclusion of all, we are practicing me-
first-ism.

Sexism is often introduced into language through the
use of a suffix. Adding *ess* or *ette* onto an otherwise neutral noun indicates a feminine adjustment to a masculine
word and is to be avoided. There is no need to use *heiress*
or *shepherdess* when *heir* and *shepherd* are perfectly
complete words.

Some ways that words are used to diminish and demean are shortcuts that imply an *ism* language, as when
an adult woman is described as a *girl*, or *tomato* or *chick*.

Likewise, using words such as *senior citizen, oldster,
teeny-bopper*, or *kid* can be put-downs to those in the
*other* age group.

## What is "Race" Anyway?

Can it be that the concept of "race" is phoney? Is "race" a
socially contrived idea that people use as another way to
distinguish between Us and Them?

In a powerful PBS documentary entitled "Race — The
Power of an Illusions," questions were raised about the
common assumptions about race — for instance, that the
world's people can be divided biologically along racial
lines. Executive Producer Larry Adelman stated that these
assumptions "are wrong. Yet the consequences of racism
are very real." The series wanted to "clear away the biological underbrush and leave starkly visible the underlying

social, economic, and political conditions that dispropor-
tionately channel advantages and opportunities to white
people." The producer added, "Perhaps then we can shift
the conversation from discussing diversity and respecting
cultural difference to
building a more just
and equitable soci-
ety."

Next time you're
in an auditorium
filled with people,
look closely. Notice
first that no two
people appear the
same. If you are
looking with an
artist's eye, you'll also
notice the variety of

> ## The Skin Color Tests
>
> A high school class recently
> conducted experiments about
> DNA and its relationship to skin
> color. What they found was —
> nothing. There is no direct
> connection between DNA and
> skin coloring. Other high school
> biology classes have learned
> that blood contains no compo-
> nents to indicate skin color.

colors — hair color, skin color, and clothing. No two
people dress the same. Each person has their own distinctive hair (color, density or lack of it, amount of curl,
length, and style. Why else does Clairol offer so many
shades of color?).

Now observe the skin. You'll see first that no one has
pure white skin or pure black skin. Most skin is a shade of
peach or brown in varying tones. Some dark skin can be
attributed to family; some is due to tanning salons. A few
years ago the Crayola people re-named their "flesh"
crayon to read "peach." Artists know all about skin color.

It is unnecessary to insert connotative reference to
cultural background when it doesn't apply to the subject.
Why attach adjectives such as African-American, black,
Asian, Caucasian, European American, native, Indian,
indigenous, Irish-American, Inuit, or Canadian, when most
of the time it is unnecessary to the topic? Other times the

adjectives are just plain wrong. If it is appropriate to use a racial distinction, be sure to make it useful. This country is coming to grips with the issue of race: the old racial hierarchy is giving way to a new multi-cultural reality.

The point: what difference does it make?

People of varying skin color live all over the world (which rules out nationalism).

The rich and the poor come in all skin colors (ruling out economy).

DNA does not indicate skin color, nor does blood (ruling out biology).

Since no two skins are identical, why is it necessary to label or try to group people by their skin tones? Let the cosmetics and medication manufacturing companies worry about that organ known as skin.

> **RACE Defined**
> "Race was never just a matter of how you look, it's about how people assign meaning to how you look."
>
> — Robin D. G. Kelley, historian

So what *does* indicate race? How can race *accurately* be defined? Which raises the question: is there such a thing as "race?" Or did we humans contrive it?

Race may be a crock — but discrimination is not. And, because humans made it up, humans can tear it down.

To avoid racist language, spend time as individuals with people whose heritage is different from yours. Refer to who they are and what they do rather than who their ancestors were. Ask about their dreams, their fears, their likes and dislikes. Then compare the answers with yours.

## Some Words Hurt (Somebody) ...

In this chapter, the preconceptions (myths) and need for demeaning terminology are dispelled. What is important to remember is that words, being *just words*, can assume meanings that aren't intended by the speaker. In truth: a *chef* cooks. A *codger* may be a warm friendly old coot, or a dolt. *Teenyboppers* go to college, or not. People considered to be *black* have as varied ethnic backgrounds as people considered to be *white.*

In some contexts the words are useful, even on target. Sometimes, however, words can become demeaning and hurtful, even when they aren't meant that way. These are, after all, just words (meaning *simply* words).

Which of the following words would you consider demeaning or belittling? When? How?

Girl ... lady ... gal ... guys

Chick ... crone ... witch ... hag ... mature

Gay ... lesbian ... homosexual ... queer

Disabled ... blind ... deaf ... crippled ...
    physically challenged

Short ... midget ... dwarf ... little people ... giant ...
    over-sized ... lanky

Fat ... over-eater ... large ... woman's size ... hefty ...
    skinny ... shrimp

Gentile ... pagan ... Jew ... Christian ... Methodist ...
    Buddha ... Hindi ... Baptist ... Muslim ... Catholic

Black ... colored ... African-American ... Afro

Caucasian ... white ... Canuk ... Euro-American ...
    Italian ... French ... German ... Scandinavian ...
    Swede ... Norwegian ... Dane ... Finn

Oriental ... Asian ... Pacific Rim ... Japanese ...
    Chinese ... Vietnamese ... Filipino or Phillipino ...
    Korean ... Hispanic ... Latino ... Chicano ...
    Mexican

Arab ... Middle-Easterner ... Israeli ... Palestinian ...
    Saudi ... East Indian ... Pakistani

Southerner ... Easterner ... Westerner ... Northerner

Rich and famous ... poor ... undeveloped ...
disadvantaged ... low income ... wealthy

How many times a day are words used — inadvertently or on purpose — to enhance one's own power by humbling another? What follows are ways humans have found to use the Us and Them Thing to demean others.

## We've Always Said It That Way

When you use a word like *man*, for instance, carefully weigh your intention. Its denotative meaning is "an adult male human." When the word is used, a mental picture is formed, a man. Why not? For centuries the word "man" has been used in reference to all humans since men were the ones who recorded language and perpetuated it.

The time has come to restrict "man" to its true meaning and seek other words to refer to all of humanity.

The Us and Them Thing is perpetuated when we use appearance to separate others from our domain — discounting someone because their skin is a different color, because they are older or younger, or because they are using equipment to help them move around easier (hearing aids, glasses, wheelchairs, or white canes).

Choosing words that exclude someone because of their appearance, even through implication, is to use words that are biased and therefore unjust. Every time we imply separation, the gap of understanding is widened.

What might help is to remember when tempted to consider someone else "out of your league," is that you are probably out of their league as well. To Americans, everyone else is a foreigner. But go to France or Japan or South America and the American becomes the foreigner. It's all perspective!

## Language Can Separate

Language reflects where it was learned. Thus, if you pick up some words from your family, some others from school and a bunch more from friends at parties, you'll find how dissimilar are the meanings of some of these words in a different context. (Do you hesitate to use your school-learned words in front of your parents?)

Endings of words — brought to American language from many other countries — sometimes try to inflict meanings that weren't meant to be there. We can call a light-haired person a *blond* or a *blonde* and (try to) imply gender. However, if you check a number of dictionaries, you'll find that in some "blond" is masculine and "blonde" is feminine. You may also find the opposite description in other dictionaries. Go figure!

If you are a student of words, you may try to pay attention to the Latin endings you learned in school. General usage now ignores many of those endings. Colleges freely use the term "alumni" to mean both male and female grads. Strictly speaking, Latinwise, *alumni* is the masculine form; *alumnae* is the feminine. You don't have to get up tight about explaining the differences. Most people would understand either spelling.

When addressing "other" people, be respectful. Look closely at the terminology you use to describe "them." If you're unsure about how to address someone, ask courteously, "How do you want to be called?" Otherwise, occupy the respectful ground and use words that acknowledge we all belong to the same body of humans, that we all are aging, that we come in two equal genders (and a variety of in-betweens), and that we have unique cultural backgrounds that may be acknowledged with pride.

Ain't this a bee-you-tee-full world!

## Patronizing Words

When are words patronizing? Some words are of themselves patronizing. Others, in condescending usage or emphasis, become so. Some of that list of "healing words" can be patronizing if they're not spoken with sincerity.

Talking down to children is a good example of conde-scension or patronization. Other patronizing includes talking very slowly in one-syllable words to an older person, or shouting at a hearing-aid wearer or a sight-impaired person, or considering the person using a wheel-chair as *disadvantaged*. Patronizing also includes talking to people of other economic classes as if they were some-how "not the same as we are": "If you were smart, you'd be rich." "If you're on welfare, either you're too dumb or too lazy to get a job."

Sexist patronization is an oxymoron, in that the root word *patron* derives from the Latin *pater*, or *father*. The dictionary definition of *patronize* is "to be kind or helpful to, but in a haughty or snobbish way, as if dealing with the inferior."

When a father talks down to a little girl, he usually is playing the domination routine, assuming the role of the powerful benefactor. The same holds true when the father figure is the male boss talking down to a woman clerk or co-worker, a male minister talking down to a woman parishioner, a male principal talking at a woman teacher, or a male sales clerk explaining "intricacies" to a woman shopper.

Whether or not the husband is talking to his wife or the brother is talking to his sister, if there is a tone of condescension (talking down) there is patronization. And yes, women can patronize too (in an oxymoron-ish kind of way).

Some patronizing phrases to consider:
*Your people suffered so in coming to this country.*
*Here, let strong hands do this for you.*
*A man of your age shouldn't have to work.*
*A child your age can't possibly understand.*
*Does the little lady need some help?*
*You may be right, in your situation, but my people…"*

Most patronizing remarks go unchallenged. They draw their abusive strength from subversion, from the very fact that because they sound good, they are not acknowledged as patronizing. Patronizing remarks are subtle, very very subtle.

Simone de Beauvoir, the French author who wrote *The Second Sex,* clarified the roots of male dominance in our culture and in our language by directing attention to the *men* who founded and developed Western religion, wrote the Bible, took charge of exploring the world in order to manage the world's commerce, established governments, fought wars and reserved education and the arts for themselves. de Beauvoir contends that to read history is to read the history of men.

Little wonder that history is referred to as the development of *mankind.* It literally disregards, sometimes by intent but surely by design, the overwhelming contributions of women along the way from cave to condominium. History disregards women's contributions to music, art, literature, government, education, athletics, commerce and religion, placing any small mention of women in single paragraphs, footnotes and sometimes in single sentences.

Language users who try to include women in words like *man* or *mankind* suggest that women don't merit their own words, that they must be content to be included in the generic *man.*

We become used to borrowing men's descriptions, men's definitions, men's titles, men's work and even men's ideas — *businessman, statesman, sportsman,* even *snowman* and *cowboy.* There is a vast difference between the meanings of *cowboy* and *cowgirl,* between *patron* and *matron,* and between *statesman* and *stateswoman.*

The result of accepting men's words in history (of men's contributions to civilization) gives off repetitious messages that women are also-rans, second-class, tag-alongs, things. For women to do anything but accept men's messages suggests that women are contentious, rebellious, mad, unreliable, uncooperative, irresponsible, insane, sick, and disagreeable.

Now repeat that message to women for a few thousand years and you see the picture that de Beauvoir saw — women who *allowed* men to "run the world." It is that basic belief still held by many women that keeps verbal abuse effective.

When verbal abuse is carried on over time by a husband, father, brother or son, a woman may grow to consider herself worthless. It may then be a small step from verbal abuse to physical abuse.

Likewise, history ignores the feats of people of color. Slavery began as a contrivance of men — another way to display wealth — through ownership of servants and control of family. Given a choice today, more men than women choose to hire servants. Hiring servants is a visible, patronizing way to help "the little woman" with her workload (and a fulfillment of social status and power).

And it all begins with words — carried down in history and through history. In this third millennium AD, at last, the implication of women's roles in society is finally being clarified by women who are demanding their place alongside men in history and in life. The importance of skin color is being challenged as well, as are the ramifications of aging, the value of wealth, and the possibilities of people with physical disabilities.

Look at the above paragraph and point out yet another discrimination. When we talk about "the third millennium," we assume we are all counting on the same calendar. Not so! Some of us are counting on Chinese calendars, or Jewish calendars, or Islamic calendars. What happens when we realize that even time has its diversity!

## Words of Love (?)

Words can heal as well as hurt. Words of hope and promise keep many disillusioned people alive during times of loss and depression.

However, some words that are meant to be kind have the opposite effect. Consider:

*You look good for your age.*

*You're so good at your job, why mess it up by asking for a promotion?*

*Some of my best friends are...(like you).*

*I so admire you people and your way of hanging in there during adversity.*

*Your husband must be very generous with you.*

*Don't you worry, you'll slim down when you find the right man.*

*You're just too pretty to have brains too.*

*You kids are so lucky not to have any worries.*

*Hi, you guys, are you ready to order yet?* (spoken to women at lunch)

*I've always wanted to know how it feels to be white (black, Latino, Asian...).*

*Is yours a Christian business?*

*I've always admired dark skin — it seems so ... tan.*

*Isn't it a wonder how they manage to get by?*

*You must come from a very good family to be able to afford clothes like that?*

Has someone made a comment to you lately that hurt just a little bit? Or a lot? What have you commented to others that may have hurt?

There will be times when you intend to pay someone a compliment and you will be tempted to use some of the words like those above. At that moment you realize your foot is in your mouth, don't try to mumble something about "that wasn't what I meant." You only make it worse by calling attention to your faux pas.

Instead, make a point of following up with this person and paying honest compliments — praise that won't be misconstrued. You'd be surprised how many things you can find to praise in another person — even when there are glaring traits that you don't like. Find them! And praise them! Haven't you learned that phrase, "I don't like what you are doing, but I like you"?

Below are some suggestions that might well be committed to memory and used often:

## Real Words of Love!

Words of love are spoken honestly, with a feeling of respect inside the speaker. Try these friendly, sincere words:

*You look good!*

*You're good at your job. You deserve a promotion!*

*I like you. Can we be friends?*

*I admire you.*

*I know you're struggling with your weight. Keep at it. You look happy.*

*Well, well, well, blessed with both brains and beauty!*

*Must be tough to be a young person these days. But you seem to be handling it well.*

*Good afternoon (morning, evening). May I take your order?*

# 7

# Don't Leave
# Me Out

## Mind Your Nonsexist…Nonracist…
## Nonageist Business

S tereotyping plays a leading role in the realm of
business, resulting in the of loss of potential dollars
when business people turn away part of their customer base with sexist, racist or ageist labels. At one time
business people addressed the "lady of the house" or
"man of the house" or wrote "Dear Housewife" or "Landlord." They soon realized that both women and men can
be heads of households, and came to know that women
make most of the buying decisions.

People of all colors, races, sizes and shapes have need
for most of the commodities of the manufacturing world.
A smart business will make its products and services
tempting and available to everyone.

The images used in media commercial advertising are
aimed toward a certain audience. Yet, by seeking a certain
segment of the buying public, a business may be overlooking and losing a large number of potential customers.
Too many ads picture a group that often includes one
woman, one black, one Asian, and three or four white
men! What this says loudly is "Trying too hard in an attempt at "equality."

In business, the subject of human rights has become so important that many companies have created an entire Human Rights Department to ensure fairness among personnel. Human rights is a broad subject that begins with the rights of free speech, religion, assembly, trial and the press. It also includes so-called rights to a home, food, a job, and medical care — for both women and men.

"The U.S. didn't invent human rights — human rights invented America," is the way former President Jimmy Carter saw it.

Women in all fields have joined the ranks of business owners and managers. In recent years the numbers of what used to be termed "men-only" jobs have diminished.

Business has also become open to people of all colors and nationalities. Ironically, in large cities, ethnic business people tend to gather to serve "their own" through neighborhood services. Neither they, nor mainstream business seems to recognize the fact that all people need health care, plumbers, good restaurants, sports equipment, greeting cards, video tapes, banking and printing services.

The world continues to shrink, causing words such as "global" and "international" to enter both our personal and business vocabularies. In keeping with the expansion of business to include participants of both genders and all races and nationalities, business language is changing too, in both form and content.

Just as styles of business management change with the times, styles of business communication — written and spoken — also change. When women entered the work force in numbers, business management (most of them) updated written correspondence stylebooks — to remove sexist language.

Sexism disappears when we address clients and staff with the knowledge that they are comprised of both women and men.

Racism disappears when skin color is ignored in filling jobs and offering promotions.

Ageism takes a back seat when employers realize that long experience equates with age, and that both age and experience are valuable assets to a company — as are youth and new ideas. Ageism works both ways.

That said, some realities of the volatile business world remain. Companies still place a larger number of men at the top; business still separates into categories, such as "black," "Latino," and "Asian;" services are still offered to "senior citizens" (as if older people change their tastes and lifelong habits as they age); workers in their 50s are still encouraged to accept early retirement, if they already haven't been downsized; young people still enter a workforce that provides a very low minimum wage.

The conundrum lies in the market that looks for separate business to cater to separate cultural tastes. The injustice lies in the market that plays on separateness — when it isn't necessary.

No, it isn't necessary to eliminate neighborhoods that enhance cultural diversity by promoting shops and restaurants that cater to specific cultural tastes. One of the greatest blessings of this country we call America is the connection maintained with "the old country," the nation of birth, the cultural heritage. While this must not be lost, we must be careful to make it fit into the stew we cherish as America. "Consider each ingredient as tasty by itself," a friend commented recently, "but so much more enhanced by the other ingredients of the stew!"

Identification of a specific market becomes a necessary part of business, sometimes called "positioning," or "targeting" or "branding." Still, many companies overlook the possibilities for sales to customers outside the customary target. As an example, auto dealers have been slow to realize the potential sales to women, especially older women. In their zeal to sell hot fast cars to 20-year-olds, they miss those whose quality cars are giving out at a time their bank accounts have grown, along with their age.

In the matter of ageism, as population increases and the number of jobs decreases, younger people are given greater responsibilities that edge out people of "retirement age" (whatever that is). Young people, eager to start their careers, flood the business world with their enthusiastic energy and a willingness to accept lower pay, thus pushing elders into the background or off the map. Too bad that businesses cheat themselves by overlooking reliable, trustworthy, experienced older people who can contribute their training, maturity and judgment to a company

The old system of "work at one job until you're 65, then retire and move to Florida," just isn't in the cards anymore. Because of economic shifts, many older people need to continue to work; at the same time, businesses are eager to push early retirement on them.

The language problem is apparent when the *Us* and *Them* words are used — when youngsters use terms such as "old fogy" and "codger," and elders use terms that refer to young workers as "kids," "teenyboppers," or "12-year-olds." All ages can find terms to recognize each other's skills, regardless of how long they've been in use. Try using these words for elders: *wise, experienced, mature*; and these for young people: *enthusiastic, eager, reliable.*

In matters of race and nationality, terms to avoid are those that belittle or demean people from other cultures. Even the term "foreigner" places someone outside the circle. It's always interesting to watch Americans in other countries when they are referred to as "foreigners." After three centuries of growth as a democracy, this country ought to be used to people of other cultures by now!

Business people may be incorrectly addressing employees as *salesmen, businessmen* or *admen.* They may be erroneously referring to the *secretary...she* or *the supervisor...he*. And why do writers cling to *Dear Sir* and *Gentlemen* to begin correspondence? How do you begin a sales letter to someone you know to be over the age of 60 — *Dear Retiree* or *Senior Citizen*? Definitely not!

Business people are skipping the "terms of endearment" that clutter up

> ## Without Words!
> While this book is about words, one cannot escape the strong messages that constantly are sent visually. Consider the images that reach other parts of the world — the ones that portray a young white macho America, a young nubile female America, and a young America composed of a large group of white men in business suits, alongside two women, one black and one Asian. Is this really America?

the beginnings and endings of their correspondence. Instead of the "Dear Anybody," use that space for a heading (*A Bargain For You* or *For The Careful Buyer* or *When You Want Quality....*)

At the back of this book is an extended Glossary of Terms to spruce up your business writing while avoiding biased language. Besides the glossary, you'll find gender inclusive job titles to use as alternatives to sexist terminology, as well as a variety of ways to refer to people of various cultural backgrounds.

## Contracts

Fields of industry are scrambling to clear up their contractual agreements (to avoid the ubiquitous *he/she* or the unjust *he*) and are also rewriting contracts to simplify wordage. Auto dealers, banks, insurance, and investment companies alike are working to present clients with understandable contracts.

Still, many contracts include somewhere in the glossary of terms or preamble to the agreement, a little clause that states in so many words: "… the masculine shall include the feminine and the neuter." *Neuter?* Then masculine pronouns are scattered throughout the document. Lazy! What such a disclaimer says is that it "covers everything that those who drafted the contract didn't have time or energy or inclination to care about." The sexist disclaimer is reminiscent of the clauses that appeared in 18th century documents about rights that "accrue to all men, excluding prisoners, the insane, slaves, women and children."

A more efficient way to solve the problem of gender bias in contracts is to go through the terminology and change all the third-person singular pronouns to genderless terms, using any or all of the suggestions regarding pronouns found in the Appendix.

How much more pleasant — never mind *just* (equitable) — it is to refer to the party of the first part as the seller, mortgagor, lender, corporation, or contractor and the party of the second part as the buyer, mortgagee, borrower, private party, or contractee! Or how about Party I and Party II?

## Emails and Web sites

The high traffic of business communication over the Internet has brought writing to a new high (and low). While instant messages fly through the air and speed up business, the temptation arises to become sloppy with the language.

Since you never know who is reading your Web site or emails, you'll want to take extra care to use inclusive language. Take as much care with email and Web site messages as you do with hard copy correspondence.

When unsure of who you are writing to, do not assume gender. If necessary, ask if Terry, Gerry, Dale, Lou, Kim or Val is a man or woman; otherwise use genderless language. Address the note with a friendly, "Hello Terry…"

While one of the advantages (and disadvantages) of on-line communication is anonymity, be extra careful with your messages. Always check spelling and punctuation. Your writing says much about the way you conduct business, whether that writing is found in a letter, a memo, a Post-it note, your Web site, or email. Make certain your messages are grammatical, inclusive, and spelled correctly.

## Names

If you haven't looked at a roster of names lately, you haven't noticed that people are blessing their children with all manner of names — names such as Chastity, Kiona, Spring, April, October, River, Illinois, Wednesday, and names with derivations from other languages.

No longer are women clearly identified with Mary, Joan, Judy or Betsy, or men clearly named John, Andrew, James or Henry. And who can remember the difference between Francis and Frances? You probably have met women named George, Michael, Andy, Marshall, even Carl, or men named Evelyn, Marilyn, and Carroll.

Some nicknames, or shortened names, loosely follow guidelines of "y" for men, "i" for women: Terry/Terri, Jerry/Jerri, Andy/Andi or Andee. But what do you do with names that seem to have no gender: Chris, Pat, Lee, Kim, Sam, Lynn or Dale?

Treat names with respect. Ask about derivations of names. Not only will you address people correctly, but you will reinforce your memory of those names.

When working with people through the Internet or sight-unseen, find out enough about them to deal with them appropriately. The best way is to treat everyone equally and courteously. That will keep you out of all kinds of difficulty.

Many names today, Asian or Middle-eastern in particular, give business people pause. Learn both to spell and to pronounce properly the names of people you work with, whether customers or co-workers.

There's a manager of a small Asian fast-food restaurant who takes time to learn and remember the names of all her customers. In return, she teaches them simple Korean words on each visit. Do they return often? You bet!

## Biased Advertising Can Cost You!

Company advertising is another place where sexist language costs a business precious dollars. When a furniture company sends out a flier offering gift ideas: a reclining chair for HIM and a cedar chest for HER, the implications are clearly sexist. How many sales are lost from women who want recliners (or men who want cedar chests).

An automobile company advertises: *We are proud to offer discounts to our valuable customers. The customer is king at our auto agency. He is treated to the best in service and quality products.* Too bad! That message won't catch the attention of many women. They don't want to be treated as "kings" and don't appreciate being referred to as "he."

Many businesses that sell high-ticket items are missing sales because they overlook women as potential customers. Business people have been slow to realize that women buy new cars, houses, jewelry, airplanes, computers, cell phones, boats, sports equipment, and furniture.

Advertising copy that automatically relegates women to the housekeeper role and men to the protector-provider role is no longer acceptable. Don't risk losing half of your customers by turning them off with sexist language. It simply is not good business.

Advertising that reflects youth as the target market risks losing the business of their families, especially the older members. The need continues for elders to buy new cars, coats, shoes, sofas, electronics, pianos, digital cameras, and vacations, yet this lucrative market is bypassed by companies trying to rope in young people — even though it stands to reason that older customers have more money than younger customers.

Conversely, there are places where companies cater to long-time clients and push away youngsters. By recognizing in youth the potential of lifetime sales (repeat business), many companies could assure their futures by paying more attention to the development of young customers.

If you are doing direct-mail business, be careful of the means you use to address potential customers. Generic terms, such as: Dear Customer, Dear Householder, and Dear Driver will successfully reach anyone, man or woman, old or young, who may want to buy your product or service. But terms, such as: *Dear Housewife, Dear Fisherman, and Dear Businessman,* or (dear God, no) *Dear Senior Citizen,* may be an annoyance to the person opening the mail.

Here are some unbiased terms you may wish to consider: *owner, leader, executive, helper, artist, assistant, developer, creator, analyst, musician, clerk, speaker, representative, builder, manager,* and *advertiser.*

## Affirmative Action

Besides all the dollars-and-cents reasons for using unbiased language in business, there are some legal aspects. Treating employees differently because of their gender, age, race, nationality or physical ability, is clearly against the law and could result in unrest (at best) and lawsuits (at worst).

Legally, when hiring, many topics are off-limits to interrogators. According to federal regulations, the following subjects are not allowed during hiring interviews: age, sexual preference, national origin, race, religion and medical history. Once a person is hired, an employer may ask about business-related matters: Are you free to work Saturdays? Can you travel out of town for long periods of time? Usually, these requirements are placed in the job description and it is up to the new-hire to be up front about availability and other requirements of the job.

Many businesses still are top-heavy with white, young, male decision-makers, while women, people of color, and older workers are clustered about the lower-paying jobs. Have you considered the role your workers play in your business? You may have noticed that the people who are in direct contact with your customers are the secretaries, clerks, nurses, teachers, bookkeepers, and tellers. Are they considered the strength of your operation, paid the best salaries, and treated with respect?

If you want a clear-cut view of your business place as it pertains to affirmative action and equal treatment, ask yourself (whether you are female or male, young or old, white or black) how your mother, sister, daughter, father, son, brother or best friend would feel working there.

## Business Associates

Another area that can benefit in profit dollars is the way business associates are treated.

Many companies that supply your business with goods and services are run by women or minorities. To assume facts about the ownership of such businesses may be costly. Chances are great that to do business with certain companies, it will require you to deal with a woman or minority in a decision-making position. Inability to deal with executives as equals is likely to result in lost business.

Women and minorities still have a long way to go in the world of business, but they are moving ahead fast — faster than at any previous time. And while average earnings for women remain less than for men, women are filling responsible roles and achieving success in operating their own businesses. You can honor leaders of business — whatever their gender, age or race — by adhering to nonsexist, nonageist, non-racist language.

## For Specific Markets

Many products and services are meant to be consumed by specific groups of people. When that is the case, use specific, courteous terms. Try to avoid euphemisms (*women/men of a certain age, boomers, teenyboppers, handicapped*).

Instead, use terms that will appeal to your audience without insulting them: women (or men) in mid-life, parents of young children, teenagers, people who are challenged or incapacitated, sightless, unable to hear, or unable to walk.

*Ableism* is a word found in publications of the Anti-Defamation League to describe the prejudice and discrimination against people with mental or physical problems.

People who are unable to walk or see or hear or use all of their physical abilities do not always feel *disabled, helpless, deficient, blind, deaf* or *crippled*. They acknowledge physical problems, but do not consider themselves "less than …," and certainly not *handicapped* (dreadful word!). Most people with physical impairments do not consider themselves either *handicapped* or *disabled*.

While *challenged* is one of those politically correct euphemisms, *challenged* is the best word to describe most of us, since we all are confronted with infirmity, ailment, impairment, illness and health impositions at times during our lives. Anyone temporarily confined to a wheelchair with a broken leg or hip ailment receives a priceless comprehension, in a small way, of the constraint experienced by those who must spend their lives in wheelchairs.

The challenge is to live life rather than focus on what could possibly hold someone back. By understanding the position of people with impairments, their challenges can be reduced.

Learn sign language to understand people who cannot hear. Learn ways to assist people who have lost the use of their eyes. Observe your environment and find ways to make it accessible to wheelchairs and safe for children and those with special physical needs.

## Real Estate

Some guidelines have been given to follow requirements in dealing with real estate, particularly the sale, rental, financing, and promotion of residential property. The Fair Housing Acts of 1968 and the 1988 Amendment cover this area of language usage in detail.

As with most areas of business, certain terminology grows up with the business. Ordinary words develop specific meaning when used in classified ads, for instance, or real estate directories. And some of them can be interpreted to exclude. The rule of thumb in print advertising is to describe the property, not the "appropriate buyer or renter, not the landlord, and not the neighbors."

A guide to help housing advertisers comply with the rules urges advertisers to watch out for and eliminate words that talk about: family, the elderly, color, religion, race or nationality, handicapped, sexual orientation, personal habits, proximity and restricted property descriptions.

Rather than describing a "home for the prestigious executive," describe it as "elegant, gracious" or "luxurious." Don't try to describe a neighborhood demographic (upscale, mid-level, senior revitalized), but focus on the property itself. Use terms like: "quiet street, quiet country living." Avoid "mother-in-law apartment" or "bachelor pad." Instead, use "accessory housing" and "single" apartment. Only when sharing living space, is it appropriate to specify the gender of roommate.

Stay away from indications that hint, "adult housing" (implying no children) or "no occupants under 62" or "senior housing" (unless it is so designated by a government program that assists the elderly). And definitely do not designate: "no children."

As owner of a property, you can set the rules (no smoking, drinking, or drugs), but you cannot describe the people (non-smoker, non-drinker, or drug-free). Stick to the property.

Ask for a list of acceptable words to use in your advertising from the newspaper, magazine, radio, television station, or agency handling your advertising.

## Hiring and Firing

Federal regulations also offer guidelines in listing job openings, job interviewing and procedures for firing employees. While they are general, state business control departments offer more specific regulations for handling Human Resources. (That term seems distant, so connected to the subject of dollar value and separate from regarding people as the most important component of your company.)

Whether the interview is to hire, review performance, or consider discharge, keep language aimed at discussing the job and the skills of the applicant.

# 8

# Grammar Police Alert!

## Illegal Word Usage

While it's not likely that some gendarme will grab you by the collar and haul you into court for using biased language, there are several guidelines that may keep you out of trouble in communicating — whether written or spoken.

One guideline is to understand the meaning of words: as *you* mean them and as *others* interpret them. Another is control of pronouns. Sounds silly, but pronouns can keep you out of "grammar court." First, let's look at the meaning of words.

### *Man* Does Not Mean *Woman*

Great attention is given in today's language to the meaning of the words *man* and *mankind*. Some contend that *man* means the entire human population — both women and men. *Mankind* likewise has been used to represent all of humanity. If you need convincing of this wrong-thinking, read "Herstory" in the Appendix.

Take another look at some other words. *Homo sapiens* is the Latin scientific identification of a biological species that includes both sexes, male and female. The word *man* in the English language specifically identifies only one of them, the male. Another word, *woman*, is used to define the other, the female of the species.

Believe it or not, we were not born with a gender word written across our foreheads. If you wish to delve into derivatives, you will find questions about the origin of the word *woman*. Linguists generally conclude it is not a diminution of *man*. (How could it be? It's two letters longer!)

Man does not mean "woman," nor should it be so used. In the interest of accuracy, biologic and linguistic: men are masculine, women are feminine.

Many alternatives are available to replace the word *man* when referring to all human beings: (*individual, person, someone*). Likewise, there are alternatives to using *mankind* to refer to both woman- and mankind collectively (*civilization, humanity, humankind, people*). Remember, there were women on that boat with Noah!

Examples:
    S:  *Man* has inhabited the earth for thousands of years.
    N:  *Humans* have inhabited the earth for thousands
        of years.

    S:  Wherever there is freedom, *mankind* will survive.
    N:  Wherever there is freedom, *humankind* will
        survive.

    S:  All *men* are created equal.
    N:  All *people* are created equal.

As demonstrated above, it is possible to emphasize precise meaning with a more accurate term. Now the reader or listener is absolutely certain the speaker isn't referring only to male people.

All human beings are not men! Therefore, to use such general terms as *industrial man, political man* and *social man* is to fall into the generic *man* trap. The history of men is also the history of women.

Avoid using *man* to refer to the typical human: *working man, man of the world, man of goodwill, man on the street.* It is just as easy — and more accurate — to use *worker, worldly or cosmopolitan citizen, peacemaker,* and *average person.*

## Male / Female

The terms *male* and *female* refer to the sex of an individual and are to be used only when referring to sex distinctions. These words are used to denote the sex of any living thing, from trees to animals, including people.

Examples:

*Females live longer than males.* (This is a bit clinical, but is accepted in biological circles. Also, the statement may be referring to apple trees or squirrels.)

*Women live longer than men.* (Better, as long as you are referring only to people.)

*Females of the human species bear the children; males fertilize the seed.*

But not:

*The string quartet includes two females.* (No, no, no!)

Better:

*The string quartet includes two women.* (Acceptable only if this is an unusual circumstance.)

Best:

The string quartet is composed of two women and two men.

## Woman

A woman is a female human, generally considered to be over the age of puberty. Younger female humans are referred to as *girls*.

Use the word *woman* as a modifier only if it is required to clarify meaning.

Example:

S: *The woman cab driver picked up the fare at Center Street.*

N: *The cab driver picked up the fare at Center Street.*

Unless there is an unusual circumstance:

*The woman cab driver picked up the fare at Center Street and was hit over the head and threatened by the man passenger.* (Note the use of *woman* and *man*, not *female* and *male*.)

Or:

*The woman cab driver asked the fare she picked up at Center Street to drive her to the hospital, where the cabby gave birth to twins.*

In American society today, some characteristics are applied generally only to women — gentleness, beauty, grace, and softness. Many men tend to reject owning these characteristics. On the other hand, many characteristics associated by usage with men, take on a completely different and more positive meaning when applied to women — *dignity, strength, fortitude, courage* and *assertiveness*. Role expectations, long held in America, are changing and no longer are being accepted without question.

Women are not asking to be called *men*. In fact, women are asking *not* to be called men — not to be included in the term *man*.

Further, women are asking that jobs and elected posts be described by terms that include women, or at least do not exclude women: *council member, legislator, sales agent, journalist,* and *business executive,* rather than *councilman, Congressman, salesman, newsman* and *businessman.*

## Describing Women / Men

When describing women, avoid describing their appearance in terms of their sexuality or femininity unless the same or equivalent terms would be applied to men in the same situation.

Not acceptable:
> *Slender, radiant, blond* (worse yet, *blonde*), *vivacious, stunning, beautiful, attractive, pert, gorgeous, lovely.*
Would you use these same words to describe a man?

When describing women, select details carefully. Honestly ask, "Would the other sex be so described?" A man is seldom described according to what he is wearing or by the color of his hair.

When referring to women, avoid using trivializing verbs, such as *ruffle, squeal, simper,* and *whimper.* Women are perceived traditionally — and mistakenly — as passive. The careful writer will not contribute to perpetuating this erroneous idea.

## Another Kind of *Man*

Not all words incorporating the syllable *man* refer to the male human. Many English words derive from the Latin word *manus,* meaning *hand* — such as *manual, manuscript, manufacture, manage,* and *manipulate.* Interestingly, the Latin word *manus* has a linguistic masculine gender. Use of these derivative words technically escape the label of sexism, although the implication lingers via reference to hands as masculine.

## Generic *Man*

Be specific as often as you can; avoid generalizations. This has always been good advice to writers. When referring to *man* as a species, use *Homo sapiens, human society, ancestors, forebears, people, humans* or *humankind*.

Other uses of *man* can be substituted by nonsexist terms.

*Man* as verb: *work, serve, operate, staff, attend, run.*

*Man* as prefix (mankind, manpower, man-hours, man-made): *humanity, human-powered, muscle-powered, work-hours, artificial.* A manhole accurately identified becomes a *utility hole.* Since we don't keep men in man-holes, why not call those things *utility holes* — which they are.

*Man* as suffix (spokesman): *spokesperson, representative, speaker.*

*Man* in the chair: *convener, president, presider, leader, coordinator, director,* or simply *chair.*

*Men* as people in general (Englishmen, Frenchmen, Chinamen): the English, the French, Russians, Italians, laity, citizens, people. (NOTE: Sometimes a guideline such as this results in unintended bias. The word *Chinaman,* while much in use in the 1800s, delivers a double whammy of connotation, not as *Frenchman* or *Dutchman* might. Use *Chinese.*)

*Men* as public servants: *representatives, members, legislators, senators, leaders, directors.*

*Men* at work: *attendants, repairers, deliverers, agents, working people, workers, laborers.*

## Sexual Preference Identity

As previously mentioned, humans are not born with generic labels. We are born with both male and female chromosomes, and also with certain sexual equipment. Scientists explain that infants carry an equal balance between male and female to about eight weeks old. That's when the dominant genes take over. Some babies are born with emotions that don't always match the equipment. Genetics places male feelings in female bodies and vice versa.

We all, to some extent, harbor both male and female faculties; it's the dominant one that determines who we are.

When a difference is not acknowledged, problems arise. *Homosexuality* is a term that refers to a sexual orientation to persons of the same sex; *transsexual* means having primary sexual identification with the opposite sex; it also means one who has undergone a medical sex change.

By understanding that humans are made of parts both male and female, it's no surprise that sometimes those parts occur in disproportion to outward appearance. Hormones, testosterone, physicality of a variety of shapes and sizes may determine the makeup of a person's sexuality.

Every day new light is being shed on this business of human sexuality. Don't draw conclusions until the facts are all known.

The language of homosexuality up until now has been demeaning: *fag, queen, sissy, lesbo, tomboy, girly-boy, butch, dyke, bull dyke,* even *gay* when used derisively.

Words play an important role in the acceptance of other humans as individuals with varying degrees of skills, ideas, emotions, physical abilities, and sexual orientation. Choose them carefully.

## About Those Pesky Pronouns

A pronoun is a word that refers to or replaces a noun or another pronoun. First-person pronouns are genderless (*I, we, me, us, our, ours*), as are second person pronouns (*you, your, yours*). Third-person plural pronouns offer no problems (they, them, their, theirs). The pronouns that give us the sexist difficulties are the third person singulars: *he, she, it, him, her, his, hers, its.*

All you have to do is commit to memory the Handy Dandy Pronoun Guide and refer to it when you need a good (and accurate) pronoun. Remember that a pronoun must represent something or someone. Always make sure who or what your pronoun replaces.

The Handy Dandy Pronoun Guide is here provided to offer a fast road to understanding how pronouns affect biased language. If you've ever had the problem remembering when to use "us" and when to use "we," you'll gain insight to that pesky problem. You'll also discover that there's only one set of pronouns that impact the subject of language discrimination — that nasty third person singular. Check it out!

Please note that in Column C, the possessive pronouns, you'll find no apostrophes. While most nouns require an apostrophe to show possession, the pronouns DO NOT (the river's edge, *its* edge; the child's finger, *her* finger; the doctors' abilities, *their* abilities).

Also note that the pesky sexist pronouns show up only in the third person column, and then only in the singular. Therefore, if you're looking for a quick way to eliminate the *he/she* or *him/her* dilemma, simply go to another line or column of pronouns! Sounds simple. Following are even more ideas for bypassing the slashy (/) words.

As long as we use the genders accurately, no problem exists. When we refer to a man, we refer to *him*. Likewise, when we refer to a woman, we refer to *her*. It's when we

| HANDY DANDY PRONOUN GUIDE | | | |
|---|---|---|---|
| **Number** | **Column A** | **Column B** | **Column C** |
| | *Doer (Subject)* | *Doee (Object)* | *Ownership (Possessive)* |
| **1st Person (S)** | I | me | mine |
| **1st Person (P)** | we | us | ours |
| **2nd Person (S)** | you | you | yours |
| **2nd Person (P)** | you | you | yours |
| **3rd Person (S)** | he, she, it | him, her, it | his, hers, its |
| **3rd Person (P)** | they | them | theirs |

*Clip this guide and stick it on your computer!*

refer to someone whom we don't know, and thus can't accurately identify by gender, that we get into trouble. There is no reason to attach a supposed gender. If you are talking about a doctor whose identity is not given, do not assume the doctor is a *he*. Find other words to symbolize exactly what you mean. Substituting the word *person* every time such a problem arises is not always the answer!

For a long time, usage has accepted masculine pronouns as "common" gender representatives for both masculine and feminine nouns. The masculine also has been used when the noun's gender is unknown or unclear. However, increasing numbers of women object to being addressed as *he*.

If you say:

*Everyone is required to carry his entry card,* you have excluded the women who need to carry their entry cards. Instead, write or say:

*Everyone is required to carry entry cards.*

Do not use:
*A teacher inspires her slow students.*
*A lawyer likes to win his cases.*
*A nurse is vigilant on her shift.*
*A police officer must keep his body fit.*

It is much better to use:
*Teachers inspire their slow students.*
*Lawyers like to win their cases.*
*A nurse is vigilant during working hours.*
*A police officer must keep a fit body.*

In English, non-living things do not have gender. Leave it out! A boat or car is not a *she!*

## Where Sexist Language Comes From

The evolution of language in America includes much usage that can be traced back to middle-European roots. Most early language usage applied only to the visible male. Men were feudal lords; men conducted business; men led religious orders; men were privy to education; men, in short, pretty much ran things.

Women were positioned somewhere down the social ladder, mixed in with serfs and real estate. They were chattels, possessions, and therefore without status as individuals, persons, or entities with rights. Women did not own real estate, operate businesses, lead religious orders or receive education. They were invisible. Even in today's United States Constitution, women are not mentioned, while special attention is paid to children, the mentally ill and prisoners. Most other nations around the world acknowledge the rights of women in their constitutions.

Contracts and other early writings excluded women automatically; women were of no legal concern in real estate or other financial affairs. Early writings therefore used only the *he* to refer to human beings in the third person, human beings who were indeed men. If women inherited or were deeded real estate, it was automatically turned over to their husbands upon marriage (after being managed by fathers and brothers until then).

## Note To Grammatical Stick-in-the-muds

A note to the grammatical purists who have trouble accepting the idea that *he* does not include the feminine. The next time you hear someone refer to "everyone … he" take a moment and look at the pictures in your mind. Are they feminine? Not likely! If you are a woman, you may also experience that old feeling of not being "one of the boys."

Not until the mid-1900s did American women claim their rights to hold property and bank accounts in their own names. In many countries, women still are denied ownership of property and other financial privileges.

Women in certain religious organizations still are refused positions equal to men.

Women in government still are discouraged from holding high public office.

Women in athletics still are admired for their appearance rather than their skills.

The subjugation of women is not confined to what sometimes are considered "backward countries" in other parts of the world; it occurs in many areas of the United States.

The idea that "we've always done it that way" doesn't carry enough weight to keep using an obviously masculine word to refer to all people, as if feminine people don't exist. The implied discrimination still shouts very loudly to too many women.

Several ways suggest themselves to avoid sexism of pronouns. No single technique will work in all situations.

The following is a menu from which to choose ways to avoid the awkward *he/she*, the overworked *person*, or other contrived sexist terminology.

— Group words to use a plural pronoun properly.
— Delete or omit the pronoun.
— Use the word *the* in place of the pronoun.
— Repeat the noun.
— Use the passive verb form.
— Change the sentence to use the first or second person pronoun.
— Use the word *one* instead of the exclusive *he*.
— Recast the sentence to change the subject.
— Use singular nouns that use plural pronouns.
— Only as a last-ditch effort, use both masculine and feminine pronouns (*he or she, his or hers*).

For details and examples of these ten suggested alternatives, consult the Appendix.

## Outdated Words / New Meanings

Not every pronoun has to be changed. When you're talking about a woman, use the feminine third person: *she, her, hers*. When talking about a man, use the masculine third person: *he, him, his*. Don't try to eliminate all pronouns, just the ones that, when used in a sexist way, tend to turn off the opposite sex (works with both women and men).

Note that language changes, especially the American English language that incorporates languages from other countries — more all the time.

Sometime, sit down and leaf through an old dictionary and see how words and their meanings change.

An obvious example of changing language is the elimination of formal second person pronouns: *thee, thy, thou,* and *thine.* Another example of usage adaptation is the *you-all* that is accepted in some parts of the country as the plural form of *you.*

Spelling English words in America changed when the colonists were intent on eliminating anything connected with their English oppressors. Hence we don't use the following British spelling: *colour, honour, favour, centre, theatre* or *metre,* among others.

The words we commonly use today in connection with the Internet weren't in the dictionary ten years ago — at least their meanings weren't. Twenty years ago there weren't too many words pertaining to computers. If you can find a very old dictionary (more than 30 or 40 years old) check out the meanings for the following words:

*gay*

*queer*

*black*

*compute*

*net*

*guys*

Don't believe that the current trend towards revising language is anything new; and don't expect the revisions ever to end. In fact, because of the Internet, new words and new meanings are being applied to words in an overwhelming number each day.

> ### Look Who Did It!
>
> Shakespeare did it! So did W. H. Auden and George Bernard Shaw and Scott Fitzgerald — often. They and other of the world's great authors used singular antecedents with plural pronouns. One dictionary even includes in its definition of *their* the following: "used with an indefinite third person singular antecedent," citing Auden's "anyone in their senses." So go ahead: follow the pros!

Over the centuries, many have tried to simplify the language — invent universal languages — simplify spelling. George Bernard Shaw tried to simplify spelling, as did President Theodore Roosevelt. At the beginning of the 20th century, President Roosevelt sought to simplify the language by accepting a list of about 300 words prepared by a special panel called the Simplified Spelling Board. He asked federal employees to adopt the new spelling for such words as: *tho* for *though, thru* for *through, laf* for *laugh, bot* for *bought, donut* for *doughnut, enuf* for *enough*. You should have been around to hear the ruckus that emanated from Congress and spread across the nation!

The irony remains. We don't have to "try" to revise the language. It is revising itself — all the time.

## *Us* and *Them*

Another problem involving unjust pronouns is the selective use of *us, we,* and *they, them*. These words are often used without specific nouns in mind. When generalizing about who *they* are, barriers are set up — fences that tend to keep some people out as much as they (fences) keep others inside.

- She did everything *they* said to do.
- *They* say that falling in love is wonderful.
- Go on, tell *them* all about it.
- When will *they* stop making a mess of this world?

Ask yourself: Who are They? Can They be defined or even identified?

Today's children live in a world that doesn't consider *foreigners* and *strangers*. Connected to the world through the Internet, today's youth are discovering that people around the world resemble themselves, even though they may speak other languages and live far away. While the human species still feels the need to classify each other (something anthropologists claim is necessary for survival), the children of the 21st century classify by race only if their society deems it important.

# 9

# A Final Bunch
# of Words

## About Us and Them

anguage is constantly changing — especially the
eclectic American language. Next time you have to
look up a word, peek at the date of your dictionary.
Very few (not enough) people replace old dictionaries
with new as they are revised. Dictionaries, once revised
every ten years or so, now can be updated daily (online),
with newly revised print editions issued annually.

In the past, change involved discarding outworn words
and adding new. Some changes (in some dictionaries) in
recent years have been made to words that previously
referred inaccurately to differences between the sexes.
This is important because language is a means of sharing
understanding. And when terminology and the symbols of
language cease to represent diminution of women and
begin to reflect equality of traits and characteristics, language usage will more accurately achieve shared understanding. While the American language still is basically a
male-dominant language, gender equality has become at
least a reasonable goal.

Many excellent books written by linguists include the
subjects of sexism, racism, ageism, nationalism, classism,

and other isms in society. Psychologists write about the effects of sexist language on young people, of racial slurs on ethnic groups, of age significance in the maturing process, and the many ways language either assists or impairs emotional responses.

The subject of slang is not addressed directly in this work — simply because the scope is so wide and fluctuating. Any parent knows that as soon as they understand what their kids are saying, the language changes. You're on your own when it comes to slang. Bear in mind the principles of unbiased language: respect and courtesy.

The purpose of this book is to offer some practical suggestions to remove the ism language from school papers, government reports, business correspondence, advertising copy, the Internet, movies, television documentaries, and other day-to-day usage. (Merciful heaven! The removal of sexism, ageism, and racism from TV sitcoms would destroy the business!)

Using language that is not inclusive can produce illegal or costly results — illegal by ignoring affirmative action programs and rights of speech, and costly by excluding potential customers — predominantly women, the aging, people of color, and people with disabilities.

Anti-discrimination legislation and regulations didn't start until the mid-1960s, beginning with the Civil Rights Act of 1967. On a federal level, the rights of several classes of people now are protected under law: race, color, sex, age, religion, national origin, and handicapped (mental, sensory or physical). State and local protection is offered in areas of marital status, sexual orientation and political ideology. Consult governmental human rights laws and regulations to see what applies in your neighborhood.

Regulations to protect a woman's rights were not always there. When Ellen Goodman, noted columnist, took her first job in 1963, she writes, "women were hired as researchers and men were hired as writers ... and that was that." She continues: "It was, as we used to say, a good job *for a woman*. If we groused about working *for* the men we studied *with* in college, we did it privately. It was the way things were." Goodman is not one to regale her audience with "the bad old days .... They already know that women were treated as second-class citizens. But what they don't know," she adds, "is that this was legal."

Some of the ism problems need time before they can be solved uniformly across the land. Careful choice of words, awareness of cultural habits, and attention to inequities will, in time, eliminate the misconceptions and inaccuracies that have been perpetuated through sloppy language usage and mindless cultural application.

How many ways can people be divided — into all manner of opposites. Try making your own list.

> pessimists/optimists
> white/black
> blue/red
> man/woman
> doctor/nurse
> boss/secretary
> master/slave
> young/old
> easterner/westerner
> physical/not physical
> Christian/Jew
> Catholic/Protestant
> Jew/Muslim
> rich/poor
> tall/short
> northerner/southerner
> academic/self-taught
> ME/YOU

As an exercise, you may receive some insight into your own way of perceiving other people. But do you really want to separate? Here are some ideas to find better ways to perceive others.

— Look for ways people are alike. After noticing the differences, look at the opposites, the similarities. Life is short and there are better ways to use your time than to ferret out human frailties of others. *We both enjoy jazz (country, R&B, rock music). We both like old movies. We're both into dancing. We all appreciate art. We love history. We all carry full class loads. We both have long hair. You and I are avid readers. We like to hang out at casinos. Both of us frequent the mall (Starbucks, KFC ...).*

—Consider your biases, your attitudes, beliefs, preferences. Listen when you use words like *we, us, they, them.*

—Allow people to sense connections with one another.

—Avoid stereotypes: *All Xs are ...*

—Correct the image behind your words by using words that translate a change of attitude and, therefore, positive action.

—Find out about others (those who may be considered as *they*). Attend multi-cultural events. Go to the Greek Festival, the Japanese art performance, a Filipino street festival, a Danish party. Celebrate every kind of winter solstice holiday you can find: Christmas, Hanukkah, Twelfth Night, Kwanzaa, Festival of Lights ...

—Instead of discussing "foreigners" or "foreign whatevers," change the idea to *people from other countries, food from other cultures, whatevers from other places, the way other people think.* The word "foreigner" always sounds so ... so ... alien.

—Think of the person *with* a disability and not *as* a disability. Use the same way of thinking when discussing people with shortcomings, with differences from yourself or your problems. They are people first ... people with shortcomings, people with long/short hair or bald heads, large people, small people, slow people, speeding people, people with problems.

Here are some more practical suggestions to ponder.

## Visualize All Kinds of People In All Kinds of Roles

You may have heard the riddle about the lawyer's child who was rushed to the hospital, where the doctor couldn't operate because the child was identified as the doctor's own offspring. (Two fathers? No, the surgeon was the child's mother.)

Practice thinking of women as having prestigious and professional roles. Women are presidents, doctors, lawyers, chief executives, senators, pilots, line repairers, . judges, police officers, mayors, insurance agents, scientists, CEOs, and fire fighters.

Secretaries, nurses, kindergarten teachers, and clerks all can be men. Managers, architects, college professors, and bosses all can be women. It is time to rethink the assumption that power positions automatically belong to men and subordinate positions to women.

Administrative roles and clerical roles likewise are shared equally with people of color, people of all ages, people from a variety of national backgrounds. It's plain illegal to restrict any group of people to or from any kind of work. Chinese don't just operate laundries; Jews don't run all the banks; Mexicans aren't all field laborers; Italians do many things besides cook pasta; all the Swiss don't yodel; the Dutch don't even own wooden shoes anymore; people of color (the phrase seems so unnecessary) are *people*. A brain isn't automatically turned off at 55 ... 65 ... or 70. Nor is it automatically turned on at 18 ... or 21 ... or 40.

## Recognize Profiling For What It Is

People of color still are regarded with suspicion in predominantly white environments. They're stopped in their cars, followed in stores, and otherwise watched in public places. Recognize that skin color does not determine character.

Profiling is not new! There was a time when speaking with a strong British accent drew attention in society, which is one reason the *American* language was established so strongly — back in the 18th century. Profiling began in this country after the Thirteen Colonies rebelled against England, when Americans sought their own language, sought to erase everything British. Ever since that time, Americans have regarded with apprehension any group that appears to threaten this country — from the early British and French, to Spaniards, to Germans and Japanese, to Cubans, to Russians, to Middle Easterners. Profiling flourished in the early 19th century when groups threatened the country economically: first the hordes of middle Europeans, then the Irish, later Mexicans, and Asians, and … the list goes on. But why profiling? Aren't these the people who comprise America — people from all over the world? Indeed, to paraphrase Pogo, they is us!

All of which makes clear the notion that "profiling" is senseless in America. Each individual "American," can trace their beginning back to another part of the world — and most make a great effort to do so. Who began race discrimination? Who decided to begin this profiling business? Even American Indians came from elsewhere, tracing their roots back across the Behring Straits … but that was such a long, long time ago.

What we call "profiling" is more accurately "scapegoating," where one group is singled out to be tormented for a time — before another group enters the picture and draws away the spotlight.

## Substitute Inclusive Words

Stay away from unnecessary masculine terms, especially those that refer to all humans. If it is important to know that the person is a man, then do so. But don't refer to "man" and expect to include women.

Avoid referring to skin color as identification. Understand that skin color does not define nationality, religious inclination, or belief system.

Be respectful of people who are older or younger than you. Remember, you were younger once, and it's for sure you're growing older each day.

Find more accurate terms to define your mental image, or remove the inappropriate term altogether. What follows are a few terms to eliminate.

Eliminate:
> color designation (*black* child)
> age definition (*60-year-old* woman)
> nationalist adjective (*Mexican* man)
> gender reminder (*woman* tennis player)

when such designations are unnecessary. A child is a child; a woman is a woman; a man is a man; and a tennis player plays tennis. Unless it is important, leave out the adjectives.

## Use Just Words

This is the bottom line in 21st century America: What we sometimes refer to as "just words" (meaning "they're only words" — the isms and other name-calling slurs) are out. Inappropriate language sacrifices friendship, harmony, money, sales, goodwill, safety, personal contentment, or all of the above.

Instead try using *just words* — those that reflect fairness, equality, respect, courtesy, harmony, and the great decency that keeps Americans strong.

## Be Aware of Confusion

Finally, if you can't go over the mountain, go around it, through it, under it, or tear it down! If you can't repair a phrase that someone may find offensive — sexist, ageist, racist, or nationalist — cross it out and start over.

Go back to the words at the close of Chapters 5 and 6 — words that help, heal, make others feel good, soothe, encourage, and that express admiration and respect. Once we are aware of the hurting words, it's a short simple step to begin to use the healing words. It shouldn't be necessary to point them out.

If still in doubt, refer to the Glossary at the back of the book.

Someone once noticed that "Sensitivity Training won't give you the answers; the trick is to be aware of the confusion."

To be challenged is to dare to become *The Other.* And most of the time it is impossible. We cannot be another skin color, age, gender, or nationality. We are who we are. To lay down such a challenge is to ask someone to be something they cannot be.

What we can be, however, is respectful of *The Other*, and courteous. Be in awe of someone who has individual traits — and thankful that includes us all! Recognize too that there is no "average," no "normal," "no ideal," when it comes to human beings. There is you and me and the rest of the world who are just like us — and yet intriguingly themselves.

Mr. Rogers said it all when he reassured you, "There is no one else in the world like you. You are special."

You are not me. I can challenge you to become me, but that is impossible; you cannot become me, as I cannot become you.

All I can ask is that you look at me. See me for who I am. Listen to me. Try to understand me.

# This is Me!

I am five-feet, four-inches. That makes me short in a world of five-feet, eight-inches, but tall in a world of four-feet, five-inches.

I am a woman, which challenges me in a patriarchal world.

I am white (actually peachy), raised in an uncolored community and living in a richly multi-cultured world.

I am educated, living among neighbors and friends who don't understand (much less agree with) all of my politics, my views, my hopes in a mediocre world, my aspirations, my work, my beliefs, and sometimes, my words.

I am past 65, living in a young world of Levi-clad youth, with baby boomers running the country, Generation X-ers cutting me off in traffic, and the media hyped on young energy. My ancestors came from Canada, France and Ireland; I am heterosexual and agnostic. Don't call me Canuk, frog, mick, nymphomaniac, heathen, shortie, old or girl!

I have been intrigued with words for many years — ever since I discovered them, in fact. I have written in many styles: journalism, advertising copy, business correspondence, magazine and newspaper articles, stage and screenplays. My books reflect my passion with words and an interest in history, including a novel. In short, I am curious — always have been.

Currently I edit the work of other writers, lead a group of these strange creatures, and I'm working on another novel — and I love every minute of it.

# Who are you?

I'd like to know. Just as Noah's wife
looked to the promise of the dove from
her mountaintop, so I too, from my
mountaintop, call to your mountaintop to
greet you, respect you, and honor you.
Maybe we can come together and accomplish something great.

## Contact:
Muddy Puddle Press
Val Dumond
P O Box 97124
Tacoma WA 98497
253-582-5453
muddypuddle8@aol.com

# Appendix

## Herstory
## Letters / Correspondence
## 10 Ways to Avoid Sexist Pronouns

*To provide the flavor of what it means to be a woman and to be aware of the words that place women in the runners-up slot of the human race, the following rewritten history is offered. Whether you are a woman or a man, notice your feelings as you read it. You may be surprised by how just words make you feel.*

### AN AWARENESS EXPERIENCE
### Herstory (History Rewritten)

We are going to reverse the generic term *man*. Think, instead, of the generic term *woman* (to include man). Think of the future of womankind, which, of course, includes both women and men. Sense that meaning to you — as a woman, as a man.

Think of it always being this way, every day of your life. Feel the omnipresence of woman and feel the nonpresence of man. Absorb what this tells you about the importance and value of being woman, of being man.

First look back to the beginnings of the civilization of woman. Remember your early ancestral relatives, the cavewomen (which includes men, of course) — Cro-magnon woman, Java woman, Neanderthal woman. Recall

137

that early woman invented fire and discovered the use of stone tools near the beginnings of the Stone Age. She also expressed her artistic self through paintings on the walls of caves. Remember that what separates woman from other species is that she can think.

Which gives us Thinking Woman, Industrial Woman, Democratic Woman, Working Woman, Creative Woman, and now even Technical Woman and Mechanical Woman. There is also the Common Woman and the Woman-on-the-Street.

Recall your past. Recall how Feudal Woman spread into Europe and built castles, how Mythical Woman developed around the Aegean and Mediterranean Seas — those mythical women who had wild adventures with strange creatures while their husbands sat at home and waited.

Follow history through Religious Woman, starting with Eve and Sarah and continuing through the crusading women. Know that the all-knowing, all-powerful God is female, as are the leaders of Her church.

And remember Discovering Woman and Exploring Woman — who had adventures sailing around the world and discovering new continents, new worlds. And recall their ships, named Nino, Pinto, and Santo Paulo (they always named their ships for men to remind them who was waiting at home).

Look now at the American Colonial Woman, those brave women who carved a civilization out of wilderness, met and befriended the Indians, then turned the men who gave them trouble into sorcerers.

Let us look at Pioneering Woman — the courageous women who crossed the mountains, fought the bears, panned for gold, built railroads, discovered oil and tamed the forests, spreading civilization across the continent.

Regard the women of art, music and literature — women who recorded life in oils and watercolors and

gave the world sonatas, symphonies, novels, and poetry
— art in all its forms. By 2002 not a single male had been
deemed a Nobel Prize laureate, and only one male act had
made *Billboard*'s annual Top 10. Only 18 men were
named in *Premiere* magazine's Power 2001 list of the 100
most influential people in entertainment.

In the sports arena, only four men made the *Sporting
News*' list of the 100 Most Powerful Sports People of the
Year 2002. The highest ranked male was 77th on the list.

Now we come to Industrial Woman, those Business
Women and Political Women who became the mothers of
our country, and the financiers, the women who sent their
daughters to war, over and over. Don't overlook Professional Woman who developed fields of medicine and law.

Understand that your physician is probably a woman,
and feel comfortable when she tells you that a body is just
a body after all. Know that your attorney is probably a
woman and that you can entrust your financial and business affairs to her. Only 12.4 percent of board of director
seats are held by men at *Fortune* 500 companies, and only
8.9 percent of board seats are held by men in second-tier
companies. Of the 280,000 firefighters in the country, only
6,100 are career male firefighters.

Recall that everything you have ever read, all your life,
uses only feminine pronouns — she and her — meant to
include both girls and boys, women and men. Realize that
most of the voices on the radio and most faces on TV are
those of women, especially when important events are
covered and important products are sold (news, sports,
comedy, advertising). At major news networks, only 20
percent of top executives are men.

Know that you have only 14 male senators represent-
ing you in Washington, and that only 65 of the 435 representatives are male. More than half the states have never
sent a man to the U.S. Senate. There have been 1,875 U.S.

senators in history; 33 have been men. Of the 26 men who have been state governors, only ten serve currently (January 2005). Very few men sit in the President's Cabinet; no man has ever served as President or Vice President; and only two men have ever sat on the Supreme Court. Know that men, including recent male candidates for the vice presidency, are oddities in the political world. Thirty years ago, men accounted for 4.5 percent of the nation's state legislators. By 2000, that number increased to only 22.3 percent of state legislative seats. Apparently men need prodding to run for public office. Women are the natural leaders, the power centers, the prime movers.

Man, whose natural role is husband and father, fulfills himself through nurturing children and making the home a refuge for woman. This is only natural to balance the biological role of woman, who devotes her entire body to the race during pregnancy — the most revered power known to womankind.

Understand the obvious biological explanation for woman to be considered as the ideal protector. By design, the female reproductive center is compact and internal, protected by her body. The male is so exposed that he must be protected from outside attack to assure the perpetuation of the race.

Thus, by nature, males are more passive than females. If the male denies feeling passive and inferior, he is unconsciously rejecting his masculinity. Therapy is thus indicated to help him adjust to his own nature. Of course, therapy is administered by a woman who has the education and wisdom to facilitate openness, leading to the male's self-growth and actualization.

To help him feel into his defensive emotionalism, the male is invited to get in touch with the child within him. He can remember how his sister could run, climb, and ride horseback unencumbered. Obviously, since she is free to move, she is encouraged to develop her body and mind in preparation for her active responsibilities of adult womanhood. She is free to train and enter the exciting world of athletics, earning fantastic sums in professional sports as well as earning the adulation of a nation's youth. Men must be kept away from sports to maintain their safety and ability to bear children.

Male vulnerability needs female protection, so man is taught the caring, less active, virtues of homemaking. He is encouraged to keep his body lean and attractive and to dream of getting married, of belonging to a special woman — changing his name to hers, replacing the stilted "master" with the respectful "mister." He dreams of cooking for her and keeping his house clean for her. If he is unable to attract a wife, he is considered unsuitable for social interaction — a spinst-him!

"I now pronounce you woman and husband" are the magical words he longs to hear. Then he waits for the ultimate fulfillment, when "his woman" gives him a girl child to carry on her family name. He knows that if it is a boy child he has somehow failed — but he can try again.

*And so life has been lived through the ages. Our foremothers paved the way for us today; we must thank them.*

**How Does It Feel?**
Are you feeling what it's like to be a woman, of being a man? Are you aware of the words that bring the ideas to you in order to evoke the feelings? They're just words — or are they?

A note must be added to this chapter before moving on. In aiming this essay at the sexist relationship between women and men, we missed the not-so-obvious racist allegations relating to *colonial and pioneering woman.* Most of history pretty much omits women and people of color (other than to mention their getting in the way of progress) — so much so that classes in Black History and Women's History had to be contrived in schools, as if the people involved were somehow separate from mainstream life.

Now re-read this feminist herstory. This time replace the references to women and men with concerns about people of color. Re-think history in terms of age. Do you realize that most of the Colonists and explorers of this continent were in their teens and twenties? That the Civil War was fought by young men and boys, barely old enough to hold a musket? That most of the wars fought on behalf of America were carried out by young fellows under the age of 30? That the "men" who sent them to war were mostly over 50?

Our views of what has gone by are strongly colored by our own background — age, gender and national heritage. Add to those interpretations the fact that the latest immigrants to the United States are the latest scapegoats. The latest "enemies" of war are looked upon with suspicion. Is it any wonder we have more than one history book to read?

Historical upbringing, however, seems to overlook the fact that white women and men "discovered" a land already well occupied by an elegant culture, and that white women and men took this land for themselves and "developed" it with their own culture. Thus they disrupted centuries of life as it was known to native Americans — the real Americans.

Ironically, and factually, all the colonists and the rest of us who followed them are the foreigners. Everyone is from somewhere else.

# Letters/ Correspondence

Change occurs in different ways for different reasons. When typewriters appeared in offices, for instance, the form of business letters changed. Later, the ease of electric typewriters resulted in letters without indented paragraphs, datelines, and closings — the block form. Amid cries of criticism, business went on, adversely unaffected; in fact, business letters using the block form are considered strikingly neat and easy to read.

Now, with most correspondence composed on computers and word processors, almost any style of letter format is possible — with ease and impact.

Yet many letters still begin and end with "terms of endearment." Heading many business letters are the ancient salutations, *Dear Sir* (even though the addressee is not identified as a sir) and *Gentlemen* (even though the addressee is known to be a company, not necessarily a group of men). Probably as old as these masculine salutations is the gratuitous *Dear Sir or Madam*.

Break old habits of letter writing by adhering to the pattern that is basic to advertising and sales people — the importance of the opening and the closing, verbal or written. The first few words set the tone; the last few words leave the message.

Use the opening words to summarize the purpose of the letter. Use a heading — across the page or neatly listed to the left side. Advertisers know that the reading eye strikes the upper left-hand corner first before skipping to the ending to see what is being asked. Therefore, conclude your letter with your request: *call immediately, send check or money order today to..., write for more information, check your calendar*, or *run to your nearest store with your money in hand.*

In other words, save your readers time. Tell them why you're writing and ask for what you want. Simple sales advice that busy people appreciate.

***Use a Reference Line*** — Starting a letter without a term of endearment may be too long a first step. If something seems to belong between the address and the first paragraph, try a reference line. Refer to an order number, invitation date, or request for information. When a letter is not addressed to a single person or department, determine its destination, and route it for more efficient handling. If unsure of the correct department title, make one up; your definition will route your letter to the right place.

Try:  *To: The Place I Can Order Your Product.*

Or:  *Attn: Person Who Will Listen To My Problem*

Move right into the letter. You can be as warm and friendly as you wish or as firm and friendly as you wish. Your message can be carefully constructed to do exactly the job you want it to.

Examples:

*Good morning, Joshua,*
*Here is the information I promised to send you*
*when we talked on the phone yesterday.*

*Yes, Marge,*
*Your order went out on Monday, just as I thought.*
*You'll be receiving it in a few days.*

*No, Terry,*
*Your order will not be shipped until we have*
*received full payment for the last order you received.*

*You have my promise, Emma,*
*You and I will meet for an interview as soon as*
*I have completed work on the job description.*

But if you insist on clinging to the "Dear ..." heading, here are some improvements. When you know the name of the addressee, use the complete name in the address, then just the name and title in the salutation:

Examples:

*Dear Mary Doe,*
*Dear Dr. Doe,*
*Dear Professor Doe* (the title spelled out for such titles as Senator, Justice, Governor, Professor or President)
*Dear Ms. Doe,*
*Dear Pat Smith,*
*Dear Chris Olson,*

The same treatment applies when addressing anyone, man or woman — just the name and title. When sending a bulk mailing to customers, the recipient can be addressed according to role or relationship to the business, as in:

*Dear Homeowner,*
*Dear Reader,*
*Dear Parent* (and please, not Mom)
*Dear Studebaker Owner,*

**Closings** — Just as old and even more stuffy are the closings found in many business letters —*Sincerely* or *Cordially yours.* How many countless hours could busy people save by omitting these senseless closings? Think how much time you would save if you didn't have to decide whether you were *sincere, cordial, respectful, truly,* or *very truly.* These terms are meaningless and usurp space. Why not close with an action-producing message, followed by your signature?

Be aware of the contents of your letter. A letter once went to a payment-delinquent customer threatening dire legal action if the account wasn't paid in full immediately. At the close of the letter were the words: *Cordially yours!*

***Business signatures*** — Courtesy titles (Mr. and Ms.) are omitted in the signature block unless there is a special reason. Occasionally, if a writer wishes to identify the gender of a name that could be either female or male, the identifying courtesy title is typed in parentheses.

Example:

*L. G. Anderson, President*

or

*(Ms.) L. G. Anderson, President*

Unless there is a reason to disclose the marital status of a female writer, the courtesy titles of Miss and Mrs. are not used in nonsexist business writing.

In short, if you must use courtesy titles, confine them to *Ms.* and *Mr.* When in doubt, ask a woman how she prefers to be addressed. And if you use *Mrs.*, use the first name of the woman instead of her husband's first name.

Business communication has been elevated to the art of coming to the point succinctly and courteously. These letters are much easier to write. Follow the same guidelines for e-mail.

All the other guidelines of writing nonsexist language apply to the contents of such letters. Avoid undue reference to *businessmen,* the company *salesmen, your secretary … she,* or *the office manager … he.*

### Sexist Business Costs $$$

Sexist language has more side effects than most of today's pills. Women exposed to constant language that excludes them tend to take their jobs less seriously. Women who feel excluded, not part of the Old Boys' Club, may neglect to make that added effort, may even sabotage their own work. Women who are not valued as employees will move to another company. Yes indeed, sexism costs money.

When women who hold responsible jobs are treated with less-than-full respect, valuable office hours can be lost. A woman manager who constantly is referred to as "the girl in charge of..." may begin to question her own worth or become angrier with each misdemeanor. Indecision and concern over status within the company often result in lost time — and therefore lost money.

Address women in business by their names and titles in the same way you would address men in their positions. Self-esteem will rise, count on it. And when self-esteem rises, so do company profits.

### Sexism in Root Words

Many words express sexism by endings other than *man*. The main culprits are word endings derived through assimilation of words from languages other than English. These endings contribute much to sexist language. And they are unnecessary.

If our language used endings to identify linguistic gender (as do Romance languages), there would be no problem. When countries use Latin-based languages, noun and adjective endings function as a major language component. In English, adjectives and nouns are not distinguished by gender. However, we do borrow some endings from other languages to differentiate certain roles and positions.

Why care about the endings of words and the effect they have on sexism? Mostly because identification of roles and people by word endings is discriminatory due to their inconsistent application. If our language used endings to identify linguistic gender (as do Romance languages), there would be no problem. When countries use Latin-based languages, noun and adjective endings function as a major language component. In English, adjectives and nouns are not distinguished by gender. However, we do borrow some endings from other languages to differentiate certain roles and positions.

Latin, which forms the base for much English, is a language that provides gender identity to all nouns in a way that doesn't always make sense. For instance, the Latin word for *sailor* is *nauta* (feminine), and the word for *farmer* is *agricola* (feminine). That doesn't mean that Latin sailors and farmers were women (although they may have been); it means the words were given feminine gender for linguistic purposes. This language quirk persists in all Romance languages (Spanish, Italian, French and Portuguese) and in one form or another in other languages.

Most formal languages have structure based on written rules (the word that this author is trying to avoid). American English has no such formal structure, which foils Americans in their wild desire to follow their love for rules and structure and labels. As a result, American English professors have attempted to formulate some kind of structure, but it is an ongoing uphill struggle, with many contradictions. The results? Fewer high schools and colleges teach formal grammar! If in doubt, ask your child's teachers how much grammar they were taught in college.

To further confuse, some of the masculine and feminine endings of other languages have been perpetuated in our usage. Words like *alumnus* and *alumna* have been so incorporated into English that the original Latin endings remain unused (except by academia) or are more often misused. Correct usage (in Latin) is *alumnus, alumni* (masculine singular and plural), and *alumna, alumnae* (feminine singular and plural), which makes *Dear Alumnus* translate to *Dear Sir*, thus excluding women graduates. It also makes *Dear Alumnas* grammatically incorrect. The increasing tendency in popular usage is to pluralize *alumna* by adding an *s* rather than the Latin *e*. (Apologies to Latin purists.) An even worse tendency is to identify all graduates (of any gender) as *alumni* (masculine plural).

The French indicate feminine nouns by adding an *e* to otherwise masculine nouns, implying that the masculine is the norm and the "altered" word applies to the feminine (*blond* (masculine), *blonde* (feminine) and *fiancé* (masculine), *fiancée* (feminine). Other French endings that feminize the norm are *euse, ette, enne,* and *ess* — all of which contributes to the sexism in the American language (*comedian* (m.), *comedienne* (f.), *masseur* (m.), *masseuse* (f.).

(Isn't it strange that current usage eliminates "masseur" and uses "masseuse" to refer to both women and men? Perhaps it sounds classier.)

In the following, use the first, ditch the second.

Examples:

usher / usherette
author / authoress
adulterer / adulteress
conductor / conductress
heir / heiress
singer / songstress
god / goddess
actor / actress
waiter / waitress

The feminine connotations wouldn't matter so much if there wasn't an economic price tag connected. *Waitresses* and *actresses* seem to earn less than *waiters* and *actors*.

Another language carry-over from the Latin is the use of the suffix *rix* to change the male *executor* into the female *executrix*, or an *aviator* into *aviatrix*. Actually, either a man or woman can handle an executor's job and both men and women can fly planes as aviators.

Note that in all of these spelling alterations, the masculine is considered the root word, or norm. The feminine form, built upon that root, is the afterthought, the addition. Therefore, by qualifying a noun with *ess, euse, ette, rix* or any other such ending, the male is indicated as the standard and the female is the deviation. Discrimination by endings can be overcome simply by using sexually neutral words, such as:

> *heir, poet, laundry worker, singer, author, waiter, shepherd, farmer, comedian, executor,* and *adulterer* (whether male or female).

Gender language is not the basis to differentiate between two qualified people. The law backs this up. A licensed pilot is an aviator; a licensed physician is a doctor; a poet is a poet; an author is an author.

# 10 Ways To Avoid Sexist Pronouns

### 1. *Group Words to Use a Plural Pronoun Properly*
When it is necessary to use a pronoun after an antecedent of undetermined or inclusive gender, try using plurals. Examples:*

    S: *A child should learn to tie his own shoes.*
    N: *Children should learn to tie their own shoes.*

    S: *The typical American knows his history.*
    N: *Typical Americans know their history.*

    S: *A Southerner likes his mint julep.*
    N: *Southerners like their mint juleps.*

Avoid providing gender to groups, thus implying a gender when it is inappropriate. All nurses are not women; all doctors are not men; all mechanics are not men; all sales clerks are not women, and so on and so on.

Use *she* or *he* only when reflected by reality. If the lawyer is a woman: *the lawyer called her secretary.* If the secretary is a man: *the secretary checked his e-mail.*

* (S = Sexist; N = Nonsexist. Please refer to the Glossary in the back of this book for alternative terms for various job categories.)

Remember: nongender terms are not used with masculine pronouns unless only males are indicated. Examples of such nongender words include: *baby, student, American, politician, Southerner, Italian, voter, slave, farmer, child,* and *parent.*

Example:

    S: *An American should salute his flag.*
    N: *An American should salute the flag.*
        *Americans should salute their flag.*

Likewise, keep in mind:

    *A sage is a wise person (not necessarily male).*
    Man did not discover fire — people did.
    All pioneers were not men.
    Half of our ancestors were women.
    *Half of the American population are women!* (To be accurate, women number more than half.)

### 2. Delete or Omit the Pronoun

In many cases pronoun are used superfluously. Many sentences may read just as well, if not better, without a pronoun. We tend to overuse these little words just because they're available.

Examples:

    S: *A voter ought to use his common sense.*
    N: *A voter ought to use common sense.*
    S: *A laborer looks forward to his lunch.*
    N: *A laborer looks forward to lunch.*

### 3. Use *the* in Place of a Pronoun

Most of us overuse pronouns. They often can be deleted without losing the idea. For some reason, we like to place possessive pronouns in front of things we own: *my* desk, *her* car, *their* house. In each of these terms, the word *the* could have been used: *the* desk, *the* car, *the* house. Of course, you don't want to overlook possession when it's important. Simply look at how you use a pronoun, and try substituting *the* once in a while.

Examples:

 S: *Mathilde mowed her lawn every Saturday.*
 N: *Mathilde mowed the lawn every Saturday.*

 S: *Jack baked his pies for the cookout.*
 N: *Jack baked the pies for the cookout.*

 S: *The bookkeeper can get used to his detailed work.*
 N: *The bookkeeper can get used to the detailed work.*

### 4. Repeat the Noun

In long sentences the distance between noun and pronoun can make for confusion. When that happens, try repeating the noun to avoid sexism. Careful writers will discover this technique also clarifies understanding of who is doing what to whom.

Examples:

 Confusing: *The judge talked to the lawyer about her situation.* (Whose situation?)

 Clarifying: *The judge talked to the lawyer about the lawyer's situation.*

 Confusing: *The clerk helping the irate customer failed to see the humor of his problem.* (Who has the problem?)

 Clarifying: *The clerk helping the irate customer failed to see the humor of the customer's problem.*

 Confusing: *Every time a doctor explained to the nurse about her temper, she failed to gain her sympathy.* (Whose temper? Whose sympathy?)

 Clarifying: *Every time the doctor explained to the nurse about the nurse's temper, the doctor failed to gain the nurse's sympathy.*

 While the repetition can seem superfluous, it's better to overuse nouns than to leave confusion about actions and results.

### 5. Use the Passive Verb Form

This technique is probably the simplest way out of the sexist pronoun dilemma. When faced with a subject that could bring up a gender pronoun, re-write the sentence to utilize the passive voice. Make the object the subject. By using a passive verb, a writer also can avoid responsibility.

Sometimes this is practiced and honed to a fine skill, and sometimes it is almost subconscious. Note the need to place blame in the following:

*Harry wrote the troublesome report and turned it over to the CEO.*

Better if Harry wanted to avoid repercussions he could word the sentence like this:

*The troublesome report was written and turned over to the CEO.*

S: *The secretary must request her time off.*
N: *Time off must be requested.*

When passive verbs are used (*was written, had been tried, is considered*) the writer avoids use of a doer and concentrates on the object.

*The report was written,* as opposed to
*I wrote the report,* or
*He wrote the report.*

If that's the way you want it, by all means use the passive. And know that this is a great way to avoid responsibility, as well as the use of pronouns. (You don't need a pronoun to identify a doer if there isn't one!)

### 6. Change the Sentence to Use the First or Second Person Pronoun

Have you noticed that the only form of pronoun that gives trouble is the third person singular? (Consult the Handy Dandy Pronoun Guide in Chapter 8.)

Well then, if the third person singular is eliminated or

ignored, sexism in language would be greatly reduced.
Notice, that doesn't say *eliminated*. Use first or second
person singular or plural pronouns. Use third person
plural pronouns. But STAY AWAY from third person singular (*he, she, hers, he, him, his, herself, himself, etc.*).
Example:

>  S:  *The carpenter must care for her saw with regular*
>       *cleaning.*
>  N:  *As a carpenter, I must care for my saw with regular*
>       *cleaning.*
>  N:  *As a carpenter, you must care for your saw with*
>       *regular cleaning.*
>  N:  *As a carpenter, care for your saw!*

>  S:  *A nurse treats his patients with equal attention.*
>  N:  *We treat all our patients with equal attention.*
>  N:  *Treat all patients with equal attention.*

Giving directions is the best way to utilize that second
person (imperative). *Do this. Do that.* There is no need for
pronouns other than an occasional *you*. Whichever set of
personal pronouns you choose, make that selection at the
start of the work and stick with it.

### 7. Use one *Instead of the Exclusive* he

Whenever you're tempted to use that third person all-
consuming, ever-popular masculine "he" or "him," and the
previous suggestions don't apply, pause a moment,
breathe deeply and try using the more formal *one*. There
are times, especially in formal writing when *one* seems to
work well. (However, it seems out of place in informal
writing or dialogue.)
Example:

>   S:  *A dancer's timing is critical; his moves must be well*
> *timed.*

N: *A dancer's timing is critical; one's moves must be well timed.*

N: *A dancer's timing is critical; moves must be well timed.*

S: *The price of grapefruit determines her breakfast menu.*

N: *The price of grapefruit determines one's breakfast menu.*

N: *The price of grapefruit determines the breakfast menu.*

### 8. Recast the Sentence to Change the Subject

Many situations arise where "you just can't get there from here." You may need to start over.

When you cannot eliminate sexist pronouns with a simple substitution or elimination, you may need to recast the sentence, perhaps the paragraph or the entire work. Don't hesitate to start over if it will remove the sexism from your writing. It is worth the effort to make certain you are not excluding or insulting any of your readers.

There will be times when you need to step back and ask yourself, "What am I trying to say here, and how can I accomplish it without excluding half the population?"

The following paragraph needs to be rewritten entirely. To try to patch or substitute words would only confuse the issue. In the interest of clear and accurate writing, this one needs a new beginning. See how much better it scans with the rewrite.

S: *Every time a farmer takes his hay to market, he finds that not only have prices changed, but the rules have changed as well. His predicament is compounded by his use of outdated equipment, vehicles he bought when he started farming many years ago.*

Some of those farmers are women. Not only does the following eliminate the sexist pronouns, but it reads better as a general statement:

N: *The plight of today's farmer is complicated. Prices change from day to day; rules change rapidly as well. In addition, many farmers use vehicles purchased many years ago when they began farming.*

What was changed in the above is the subject: from *a farmer* to the *plight of today's farmer.* Thus the plight is emphasized and a stronger statement evolves.

An easier way to rewrite is to include a modifying phrase or clause to accommodate exclusive pronouns. Example:

S: *If a reader needs a good book, he goes to the library.*
N: *A reader who needs a good book goes to the library.*

There are other ways to eliminate sexist pronouns — those pesky little words that tend to turn off half the population. One is to re-word the sentence by changing the subject. As with the example of the farmer (above), change the object into the subject:

Instead of:

*The tailor puts in ten hours of his time to complete his work.*

*The musician can complete his recording easier with the help of an amp.*

Try:

*A suit takes ten hours for a tailor to complete.*
*An amp improves a musician's recording.*

### 9. Use Singular Nouns With Plural Pronouns

Many of the world's great authors have used singular antecedents with plural pronouns. (Ooh the gasps!)

Today's language is considerably different from the language of our ancestors, simply because language changes and develops as people use it. So don't climb on a high horse and exclaim, "But the pronoun has to match the noun it replaces in number!" Sure, there was a time when grammar teachers placed their large red marks on school papers that contained such sentences as

*"Every ball player needs their own mitt."*

Or, *"Any student can write their own essay."*

Many still do, and that's okay for the formal instruction of grammar. But when you reach usage, the grammar "rules" relax a bit and stretch into guidelines.

You see, this is what has happened. Linguistics professors have determined that language is a natural instinct of humans. Wherever you go in the world, people have a language. And most of those languages come with a set of (humanly contrived) "rules." However, some of the more primitive tribes have only a spoken language (structured as it may be). But when people (French, Spanish, German, Chinese, Russian, Vietnamese, even aboriginal) come to this country, they mix their native language with what they find here — English and French in the beginning, more recently a variety of Asian tongues, and more and more inclusive of all languages.

As a result, our American English language has become very unstructured. We talk a good bit, but the "rules" have been entwined, clouded, even discarded, over the years with usage.

For the record, the author is a user of language — not one of those linguistics professors — and therefore is aware of the language as it is used, rather than as it has been constructed. That leaves us with some guidelines, and a myriad of exceptions. Remember Miss Miller in school telling you "the rule," then adding "the exceptions"? That's because there exists controversy as to exactly which rules to follow. (Consider the comma. Whole books have been written about it — and there still is controversy.)

For years, teachers told you to match the pronoun number with the antecedent (the word it represents). And they mostly used the masculine pronoun to do it:

*Every child loves his mother.*

Now, thanks to many recognized language authorities, grammarians accept the plural pronoun with the singular antecedent. *Every child loves their mother.* (Miss Miller just fainted.) Strong precedents have been established by authors such as William Shakespeare and George Bernard Shaw who used the pronouns *they, their* and *them* following such words as *every, any, each*, and *some*, as well as after other singular nouns.

*Someone shouted their concern.*

*Whoever decided on red aprons needs their head examined.*

To avoid misunderstanding, look closely at your sentence. Is it clear? If the pronouns result in inaccuracy (which this one does — *Every child loves their mother*) — you may need a last-ditch effort to use the compound (*Every child loves his or her mother*). This sentence would more accurately be written: *All children love their mothers.*

Sexist Example:

*Every participant is responsible for his own materials.*

Nonsexist:

*Every participant is responsible for their own materials.*

More accurate:

*Every participant is responsible for his or her own materials.*

Less awkward:

*Participants are responsible for their own materials.*

The following would be smiled upon approvingly by Mr. Shakespeare, et al:

*Each one attending should have their own notebook.*
*Anyone can present their idea in public.*
*Who wants to read their report first?*
*Someone has provided more than their share.*

## 10. The Last-Ditch Effort

As observed earlier, language guides follow usage and not the other way around. Language is used before it appears in dictionaries and rulebooks. Sometimes we believe that language can be forced into usage, but this seldom works. (Remember Esperanto? Conceived in an attempt to form a universal language, it never took hold.)

Early attempts to come up with a nonsexist third person pronoun (other than *it*) haven't worked either, mostly because the solutions were either unpronounceable or extremely obscure.

Occasionally in writing, as a last-ditch effort to salvage a sentence from sexism, multiple pronouns (his/her, (s)he) can be used. But, please, only as a last-ditch effort. Example:

*A mechanic must conduct business according to his or her own standards.*

Often seen, but less desirable:
*The attitudes of a business owner are reflected in his / her employees.*
Or: *Whether or not a barber is successful depends upon the way (s)he treats the customer.*

Ultimately, we're left with a few general guidelines for handling sexist pronoun situations:
—make the pronouns plural,
—replace them,
—eliminate them,
—or rewrite to avoid them.

# Glossary
# Of Alternative Terms

| | |
|---|---|
| actress | actor |
| adman | advertising agent, representative, ad person, creator, planner, layout person, adsmith, artist |
| administratrix (*Law*) | administrator |
| adulteress | adulterer |
| advanceman | advance agent |
| adventuress | adventurer |
| African-American | American |
| Afro-American | American |
| aircraftsman | aviator, aircraft engineer, rocket engineer |
| airline stewardess | airline steward, flight attendant |
| airman/woman | pilot, aviator, flyer |
| airmanship | flying skill, aviation skill |
| alderman | public official, council member |
| alumna, alumnae (*Latin*) | (do not use to include men) |
| alumnus, alumni (*Latin*) | (do not use to include women) |
| Amazon (woman) | *derogatory* |
| ambassadress | ambassador |
| anchorman | anchor, reporter, editor, news reader |
| ape-man | pre-human, missing link |
| Arab | Middle-Easterner, Palestinian, Israeli, Iraqi, Saudi, Muslim, etc. |

| | |
|---|---|
| assemblyman | assemblyperson, assembly member, assembler, assembly worker, legislator |
| authoress | author |
| aviatrix, aviatress | aviator, pilot, flyer, ace, space jockey |
| baby (woman) | *derogatory* |
| baby doll (woman) | *derogatory* |
| bachelor girl / bachelorette | single woman, unmarried woman |
| bachelor pad | single apartment, accessory housing |
| bachelor's degree | undergraduate degree |
| bag (woman) | *derogatory* |
| bagboy | bagger, grocer's assistant/helper |
| baggage man | porter, checker |
| bailsman | sponsor, bailer, bailperson |
| ball and chain (woman) | *derogatory* |
| ballerina | ballet dancer |
| bandsman | instrumentalist, band player, band member (flutist or trumpeter) |
| barman/maid | bartender, barkeep, waiter |
| barmaster (*Brit.*) | chancellor, squire, jurat, recorder |
| bastard (epithet) | *derogatory* |
| bastard (child of unknown parentage) | *eliminate* |
| bat (woman) | *derogatory* |
| bathing beauty | *derogatory* |
| batman (*Brit.*) | orderly |
| battle-ax (woman) | *derogatory* |
| beauty queen | *demeaning* |
| beaver (woman) | *derogatory* |
| bedfellow | partner, associate, mate |
| bellboy | bellhop, porter, messenger, helper |
| better half (woman) | *derogatory* |
| biddy | woman |
| big man | personage, person of importance or greatness |
| bird (Br.) | woman |
| birdman, man-bird | aviator, pilot, flyer |

| | |
|---|---|
| bitch (woman) | *derogatory* |
| black | person of color (if necessary) |
| black widow (woman) | *derogatory* |
| blind | (see below) |
| blind man | person without sight, blind person, unseeing person, visually impaired individual |
| blonde | blond |
| blushing bride | bride |
| boardman | member of the board |
| boatman | boater, rower, sailor, captain |
| bondsman | guarantor, insurer, bondsperson |
| bookman | scholar, author, librarian |
| bossman/lady | boss, owner, partner, president |
| bowman | archer, shooter |
| boyfriend (man) | friend, companion, partner |
| boyish | youthful |
| brakeman | guard, railroad worker |
| brave (n.) | young man, native American |
| Braves | (*eliminate* as sports title) |
| brethren (unrelated) | laity, congregation, assembly |
| brewmaster | brew director, chief brewer, head brewer |
| bridesmaid | bridal attendant |
| broad (woman) | *derogatory* |
| brother (unrelated) | friend, cohort, companion |
| brotherhood | human kinship, camaraderie, community, esprit de corps |
| brotherly | friendly, kind |
| brotherly love | goodwill, charity, altruism, bigheartedness |
| brunette | brunet |
| buck (man) | *derogatory* |
| bull (man) | *derogatory* |
| bull dyke | derogatory |
| bull session | meeting, get-together, talk-fest |
| bum | homeless person, street person, someone in need |
| bunny (woman) | *derogatory* |
| busboy | service worker, waiter's helper |
| bushmen | people of the bush or outback |

| | |
|---|---|
| businessman/woman | executive, financier, entrepreneur, industrialist, tycoon, magnate, capitalist, leader, manager, owner, partner, businessperson (also field of business, e.g., accountant, broker, marketer, agent, designer, architect, journalist, retailer, etc.) |
| busman | bus driver |
| busman's holiday | vacation, long holiday |
| butch (n.) | lesbian |
| butch (adj.) | *derogatory* |
| cabin boy | crew member |
| cabman | cab driver, cabby, hack |
| call girl | sex worker |
| cameraman, camera girl | camera operator, photographer, video technician |
| Canuk | Canadian |
| career girl | career person, careerist, professional, or career woman to differentiate from career man |
| cat (woman) | *derogatory* |
| cattlemen | cattle breeders, cattle owners, cattle herders |
| catty (woman) | *derogatory* |
| Caucasian | Westerner, light-skinned |
| cavemen | cave dwellers, cave people (appropriately defined, e.g., Neanderthal, Cro-Magnon, Australopithecus) |
| chairman (verb) | chair, preside, administrate, officiate |
| chairman (noun) | chair, presider, leader, speaker, convener, coordinator, facilitator, head, lead officer, director, administrator |
| chambermaid | housekeeper, servant, personal attendant |
| charwoman | charworker, janitor |
| checkroom girl | checkroom attendant |
| chessman | chess piece (rook, castle, pawn, etc.) |

| | |
|---|---|
| Chicana/Chicano | use appropriately with person of Mexican background |
| chick (woman) | *derogatory* |
| chickie-baby (woman) | *derogatory* |
| chief | head of state, leader, director |
| Chiefs | (*eliminate* as sports title) |
| Chinaman | Chinese person, man/woman of Chinese birth |
| chink | *derogatory* |
| chippie (woman) | *derogatory* |
| choirgirl/boy | choir member, singer |
| chore boy/girl | messenger, helper, attendant |
| chorus boy/girl | member of the chorus, dancer, singer, performer |
| Christian | use in religious context |
| churchman | churchwarden, elder, lay officer, acolyte |
| cigarette girl | cigarette vendor |
| city fathers | city council, leaders, founders, officeholders |
| clansman | member of the clan |
| classman | student, pupil, trainee |
| cleaning lady | house cleaner, janitor, housekeeper |
| clergyman/woman | pastor, minister, member of the clergy |
| clinging vine (woman) | *derogatory* |
| clubwoman/man | socialite, member |
| coachman | driver |
| coastguardsman | cadet, middy, coast guard |
| coed | student |
| colored man/woman | person of color |
| comedienne | comedian, comic, humorist |
| committeeman/woman | committee member |
| common man | commoner, average person |
| company man | team player, loyal employee |
| concertmaster | first violinist, concert leader |
| conductress | conductor |
| confidante | confidant |
| confidence man | confidence-game player, cheat, swindler |
| con man | con artist |

| | |
|---|---|
| Congressman/woman | Member of Congress, Representative, Senator |
| contact man | contact person, liaison |
| coon | *eliminate* in reference to people |
| copy girl/boy | copy carrier, messenger |
| copyman | copy editor, copy writer, copy chief |
| coquette | *derogatory* |
| costerman (*Brit.*) | costermonger, vendor, peddler, hawker |
| councilman | council member, councilor, representative |
| counterman/girl | clerk, waiter |
| countryman | compatriot, citizen, patriot |
| cow (woman) | *derogatory* |
| cowboy/girl/man | cowhand, cowkeeper, rider, cowpoke, cowpuncher |
| Cowboys & Indians (game) | seek and find, hide and seek |
| cracker (person) | *eliminate* or use southerner |
| craftsman | artist, artisan, skilled worker, accomplished crafts worker |
| craftsmanship | skilled artistry, craft ability, experience, accomplishment, craftship (like authorship), handcraftship, artisanship |
| crewman | crew member |
| crippled | *eliminate*; use: person in wheelchair, person who uses a wheelchair, person who lost a leg, |
| crone (woman) | *eliminate* as a derogative. Crones are wise women! |
| dairyman | dairy farmer, dairy worker, herder, dairy delivery driver |
| dame (untitled woman) | *derogatory* |
| dancing girl | dancer |
| danseuse | danseur, dancer |
| dayman | day worker, day laborer |
| deaconess | deacon, elder |
| deaf | person who cannot hear |
| dear, dearie | use only in intimacy |
| dear sir | *eliminate* as letter salutation |

| | |
|---|---|
| debutante | one making a debut |
| deep-sea man | saltwater sailor, deep-sea sailor, deep-sea diver |
| deliveryman | delivery person, deliverer |
| developmentally disabled | use in medical context only |
| directress | director |
| disabled | person with hearing loss, sightless, person in wheelchair, person without use of legs |
| dish (woman) | *derogatory* |
| distaff | *eliminate* in reference to women |
| divorcée | divorcé |
| dog (woman) | *derogatory* |
| doll (woman) | *derogatory* |
| doorman | door attendant, doorkeeper, porter, bell captain, valet |
| doughboy | soldier |
| draftsman | drafter, draftperson, drawer |
| drayman | wagoner, trucker |
| drum major/majorette | baton twirler, band leader |
| dustman (*Brit.*) | street sweeper |
| Dutchman | Dutch person, native of the Netherlands |
| dwarf | *(use only with permission of little person)* |
| dyke | homosexual, lesbian |
| elderman | elder |
| elder statesman | senior political leader, senior government leader |
| element's daughter (*Chem.*) | offspring or descendent element (elements of radioactive decay) |
| emperor, empress | ruler, monarch, sovereign, regent, commander, leader |
| enchantress | enchanter, charmer, tempter |
| engineman | engineer, engine driver |
| Englishman | English person |
| enlisted man | enlistee, recruit, member |
| equestrienne | equestrian, rider |
| errand boy | messenger, courier |
| exciseman (*Brit.*) | tax collector |
| executrix (*Law*) | executor, administrator |

| | |
|---|---|
| expressman | deliverer, transporter |
| exterminator man | exterminator |
| | |
| faggot/fag | homosexual, gay |
| fair sex | *derogatory* |
| fallen woman | *derogatory* |
| fall guy | scapegoat, stand-in |
| family of man | humankind, the human family |
| fancy man | gay, sex worker |
| fancy woman | sex worker |
| farmerette | farmer |
| fashion plate (woman) | *derogatory* |
| fat | *avoid in referring to people* |
| father/master God | Creator, Parent, Protector, Almighty Being, Power, Love, Holy One, God, Spirit |
| Father of Waters | Mississippi River |
| fatherland | homeland, native land |
| faultsman | troubleshooter, maintenance person |
| favorite son | favorite, candidate |
| feeble | weak |
| feeble-minded | dementia |
| fellow | friend, comrade, associate, peer, mate |
| fellowman | kindred human being |
| fellowship | foundation, provider, stipend, gift, fund |
| feminine rhyme (Poetry, Music) | rhyme with an unstressed final syllable |
| ferryman | ferryer, ferry operator |
| fiancée | fiancé, betrothed, affianced |
| fickle | *eliminate as a description of women* |
| fighting man | soldier, fighter |
| filly (girl) | *derogatory* |
| fireman | fire fighter |
| first lady | President's spouse, refer to by name: Abigail or Ms./Mrs. Adams |
| fisherman | fisher, marine farmer, aquaculturist, angler, |
| fishwife | *derogatory* |

| | |
|---|---|
| flag girl/man | flagger, train guard, signaler |
| floorman/lady | floor walker, stockbroker |
| flower girl | flower attendant |
| fluff (girl) | *derogatory* |
| flyboy | pilot, flyer, aviator |
| footman | valet, servant |
| forefather | forebear, ancestor, foreparent, founder |
| forelady/man | supervisor, overseer, chair, spokesperson, superintendent, jury foreperson, leader |
| forgotten man | the unemployed, the poor, the underprivileged, the destitute |
| founding father | founder, trailblazer, pioneer, innovator, forebear, ancestor |
| fox (woman) | *derogatory* |
| fraternal twins | non-identical twins |
| fraternity | social men's club |
| fraternize | socialize, associate with, consort with |
| freeman | free person |
| Frenchman | French person, native of France |
| freshman | beginner, first-year student, novice, initiate |
| frog | eliminate in reference to French person |
| frogman | diver, sailor, swimmer |
| frontiersman | pioneer, leader, settler, forester, forerunner, explorer |
| front man | mediator, intermediary |
| fruit | *eliminate* in reference to people |
| funnyman | comedian, humorist, comic |
| G-man | government employee, agent, police officer, detective |
| gagman | writer, humorist |
| gal | (a pronunciation of girl) use only for girls under 14 |
| gamesmanship | game playing |
| garbageman | recycler, garbage/trash collector, waste management engineer |
| gasman | gas deliverer, attendant; anaesthesiologist |

| | |
|---|---|
| gateman | gatekeeper, gate tender, security guard |
| gay | acceptable reference to homosexual person |
| geisha girl | geisha, dancer |
| Gentile | non-Jewish |
| gentleman | use on par with lady |
| gentlemen | avoid as letter salutation |
| gentlemen's agreement | honorable agreement, handshake, unwritten pact |
| giant | large person, big person |
| girl | young woman under 14, not a thing (animal, boat, car, etc.) |
| girl (or gal) Friday | secretary, assistant, receptionist |
| girlfriend (woman) | friend |
| girlie | *derogatory* |
| girlie boy | *derogatory* |
| girlish | youthful |
| glamor girl | *derogatory* |
| goddess | god |
| godfather/mother | *use as appropriate* |
| God the Father | See father/master God |
| golden ager | senior, elder |
| goodwife | wife, spouse, partner |
| gossip (woman) | *derogatory* |
| governess | children's caretaker/nurse/sitter |
| gownsman | gownsperson, professional or academic person |
| grandfather clause | existing-condition clause |
| grandfather/mother | use as appropriate |
| granny shoes | describe the shoes |
| granny | use only as endearing term for grandmother |
| gray mare (woman) | *derogatory* |
| great man | great person, celebrity, personage, benefactor |
| groceryman | grocer, clerk |
| guardsman | guard, soldier |
| guildsman | guild member, guildsperson, union member, cardholder |
| gunman | shooter, killer, assassin, hoodlum, gunner |

| | |
|---|---|
| guy (woman) | *eliminate* |
| gyp (n.) | frawd, swindle |
| gyp (v.) | defraud, swindle |
| | |
| hackman | hackie, cab driver, cabby |
| hag (woman) | *derogatory* |
| handcraftsman | handcrafter, handcraft person, artist |
| handmaid | instrument, tool, agent, vehicle, medium |
| handyman | helper, handyperson, carpenter, plumber, electrician |
| hangman | executioner |
| hardwareman | retailer, hardware seller, clerk |
| harlot | *derogatory* |
| harpy (woman) | *derogatory* |
| hat-check girl | hat-check attendant, hat checker |
| hatchetman | hanger-on, killer, hoodlum, roughneck |
| he/she or her/him | See Appendix |
| headman | boss, owner, president, supervisor, manager |
| headmaster | principal |
| hefty | large person |
| heifer (woman) | *derogatory* |
| heiress | heir |
| helmsman | coxswain, guider, steerer |
| he-man | man |
| hen (woman) | *derogatory* |
| henchman | right-hand helper, follower, adherent, flunky, hanger-on, women's party |
| hen party | |
| hen-pecked | *derogatory* |
| herdboy, herdsman | herder |
| heroine | hero |
| helmsman | pilot, guide, steerer, navigator |
| highwayman | robber, thief, vandal |
| hillbilly | southerner, mountain person |
| Hispanic | use appropriately with someone of Spanish background; commonly used as a broad term for Spanish speaking people. |

| | |
|---|---|
| history of man | history |
| hobo | wanderer, homeless person |
| holdup man | robber, thief, mugger |
| homo | homosexual |
| honey | use only in intimacy |
| hooker (woman) | sex worker |
| horseman | horseback rider, trainer, horse breeder, equestrian |
| horsemanship | ridership, equitation, skill |
| hostess | host, attendant, social director |
| hotelman | hotel operator, manager, desk clerk |
| househusband | homemaker, householder |
| housewife | homemaker, householder |
| hoyden | active child |
| hula girl | hula dancer |
| hunk (man) | *eliminate* |
| huntress | hunter |
| huntsman | hunter |
| hussy | *derogatory* |
| ice cream man | ice cream vendor, seller |
| idea man | idea person, creator, imaginative person |
| illegitimate | *eliminate in reference to children* |
| Indian clubs | workout equipment |
| Indian | Native American, American Indian, East Indian, native (*eliminate* as sports title) |
| industrial man | industrialist |
| infantryman | infantry soldier, foot soldier |
| inner man | inner self, inner person, psyche, spirit |
| inside man | accomplice, undercover agent, spy, insider |
| insurance man | insurance agent, representative |
| Irishman | Irish or Irish person |
| jack and jill (*Brit.*) | showers |
| jack-of-all-trades | handy person, handy worker |
| Jap | Japanese |
| jazz man | musician, jazz player |

| | |
|---|---|
| Jew | Jewish person |
| jew down (v.) | negotiate, dicker, barter |
| Jewess | Jewish person; |
| Jezebel (woman) | *derogatory* |
| jiggle (woman) | *derogatory* |
| john | man who buys sex |
| john | toilet, water closet, bathroom, restroom |
| johnny-on-the-spot | prompt person |
| johnny-come-lately | newcomer, new arrival, recruit |
| John Q. Public | the public |
| journeyman | experienced worker, journey-level (mid-level) tradeworker |
| junior miss | *eliminate* |
| juryman | juror, member of the jury |
| just like a woman | *eliminate* |
| kept woman | *derogatory* |
| kewpie doll (woman) | *derogatory* |
| key man | key person, key executive |
| kike | *derogatory* |
| kinglike | regal, dignified, noble |
| kingmaker | politically powerful person |
| kingpin | political leader |
| king's English | proper English |
| king-size | large, huge |
| king's ransom | valuable goods, huge sum |
| kinsmen | kin, kinfolk, relatives |
| kitten (woman) | *derogatory* |
| ladies' man | *derogatory* |
| Lady Luck | luck, good fortune |
| Lady Nicotine | tobacco, bad fortune |
| lady (adjective) | *eliminate* |
| lady-killer | *derogatory* |
| ladykin | *derogatory* |
| ladylike | define |
| lady of the evening | *derogatory* (use sex worker) |
| lady of the house | *derogatory* |
| lady's auxiliary | auxiliary |
| lady's wind | gentle breeze |

| | |
|---|---|
| landlord/lady | owner, manager |
| Latino | person of Latin background |
| laundress, laundryman | laundry worker |
| lawman | officer, sheriff, lawkeeper, enforcer, police officer |
| layman | lay person, laity |
| layout man | layout person, designer |
| leading man/lady | leading actor, star |
| leadman | leader |
| learned man | learned person, sage, scholar |
| leg man | runner, messenger, reporter |
| lesbian | homosexual woman |
| lesbo | *derogatory* |
| letterman | athlete of achievement, achiever |
| lighthouse man | lighthouse keeper |
| lineman | line installer, line repairer, line worker, electrical technician; train worker; football player |
| lioness | lion |
| little lady | *derogatory* |
| little person | *(use only with permission of dwarfed person)* |
| little woman | wife |
| longshoreman | stevedore, dock hand, loader |
| lookout man | guard, sentry, lookout |
| loose woman | *derogatory* |
| low man (on the totem pole) | neophyte, beginner |
| lumberman, lumberjack | logger, woodcutter, forester |
| madam | *derogatory* |
| madame | French term for woman |
| madman | lunatic, maniac, mentally ill |
| maid | houseworker, servant, attendant, domestic |
| maiden | untried, first, early, single |
| maidenhood | girlhood |
| maidenly | *derogatory* |
| maiden name | father's name, family name, birth name |
| maid of honor | honored attendant, best woman |
| mailman | postal carrier, mail carrier, letter carrier |

| | |
|---|---|
| maintenance man | janitor, repair technician, upkeep technician |
| maitre d' | dining-room captain, head waiter |
| majorette | major |
| make a new man | make a new person |
| makeup man | makeup person, makeup artist, cosmetician |
| male/female hardware | couplings; plugs and sockets |
| mama's boy | favorite child |
| man (noun) | use to refer to male person |
| man (verb) | operate, tend, staff |
| man about town | roue, single man, popular man |
| manageress | manager |
| man among men | important person |
| man and wife | wife and husband, husband and wife, man and woman, woman and man |
| man eater | cannibal, savage, carnivorous |
| man Friday | servant, attendant, assistant |
| manful, manfulness | *define* |
| man from Mars | creature from Mars, alien |
| man from outer space | creature from outer space, alien |
| manhandle | mishandle, maltreat, abuse |
| manhole | utility hole, maintenance hatch, sewer, conduit |
| manhunt | search, investigation |
| man hours | work hours, time |
| man in the street | average person, person in the street, common person |
| mankind | humankind, humanity, civilization, people |
| manlike | anthropomorphic, humanlike |
| manly, manliness | *define* |
| manmade | synthetic, artificial |
| mannish | *define* |
| man of action | human, dynamo, hustler, go-getter, enthusiast |
| man of God | minister, pastor, holy person, priest, rabbi, imam |
| man of goodwill | peacemaker |
| man of letters | academic, scholar |
| man of means | person of means, rich person |

| | |
|---|---|
| man of straw | nonentity, insignificant person |
| man of taste | person of taste, sophisticate |
| man of the hour | honored person, VIP |
| man of the world | cosmopolitan, citizen of the world, sophisticate |
| man of the year | honored person, citizen of the year |
| man-of-war | armed naval vessel, warship |
| man on horseback | dictator, tyrant |
| man on the street | common person, average person |
| man overboard | someone's overboard, help! |
| manpower | labor, work crew, staff, personnel, human power, muscle power |
| man's best friend | dog |
| man-sized | large |
| man's law | the law |
| man's work | work |
| man-to-man | face-to-face, one-on-one, person-to-person |
| mare (woman) | *derogatory* |
| marked man | marked person, target |
| marksman | shooter, sharpshooter, crack shot, dead-eye |
| marksmanship | shooting proficiency |
| masculine rhyme (*Poetry, Music*) | rhyme with a stressed or strong final syllable |
| masseuse | masseur, massager, massage therapist |
| master (n.) | expert, specialist |
| master (v.) | to achieve excellence |
| master/father | (See *father*) |
| masterful | skillful, imperious, arrogant |
| master key | skeleton key, passkey |
| mastermind (n.) | leader, planner, creator |
| mastermind (v.) | to create |
| master of ceremony | announcer, leader, coordinator, emcee |
| masterpiece | great work of art |
| master plan | blueprint, ground plan, working plan, plan of action, project design |

| | |
|---|---|
| master's degree | graduate-level degree |
| master stroke | bright idea, brilliant move |
| matron of honor | honored attendant, best woman |
| mayoress | mayor |
| meatman | butcher, mean cutter |
| mechanical man | robot, mechanical device, machine |
| medical man | doctor, medical practitioner, physician, health care worker |
| medicine man | spirit healer, doctor, native doctor, shaman, faith healer |
| men | refer only to masculine humans |
| men working | people working, workers ahead, workers, work party |
| meter man/maid | meter reader, attendant |
| metropolitan man | sophisticate, urbanite |
| mick (Irish) | *derogatory* |
| middleman | negotiator, go-between, liaison, intermediary, contact person |
| midget | small person, little person |
| midshipman | cadet |
| milady | describe |
| militiaman | soldier, cadet |
| milkman | milk deliverer, dairy worker, milk-truck driver |
| minority | *careful who and how you count* |
| Miss | Ms. |
| missy | *derogatory* |
| mistress | *eliminate (unless using equal term for men)* |
| modern man | people today, modern humans |
| molly (man) | *derogatory* |
| mother country | native country, homeland |
| Mother Earth | earth, world, globe, planet |
| motherhood, fatherhood | parenthood |
| mother-in-law | eliminate in jokes |
| mother-in-law apartment | accessory housing, single apartment |
| motherland | native country, homeland |
| motherlike | describe |
| mother lode | main lode, major vein |
| Mother Nature | nature |

| | |
|---|---|
| mother's son | parent's child |
| mother tongue | native tongue, native language |
| motorman | driver; engineer |
| Mrs. | Ms. |
| murderess | murderer |
| | |
| nag (woman) | *derogatory* |
| nanny | children's caretaker, nurse, sitter |
| Native American | American Indian |
| needlewoman | needleworker, sewer |
| Negress | woman of color |
| Negro/Negroid | person of color |
| new man | new person |
| newsboy | news deliverer; news seller, news carrier |
| newsman | reporter, anchor, journalist |
| newspaperman | editor, reporter, journalist, copy writer |
| nigger | *derogatory* |
| night watchman | night guard, security guard, sentry |
| nigro | *derogatory* |
| nobleman | nobleperson, member of the nobility |
| no man's land | unowned or uninhabited land, the wild |
| Norseman | Norse person, Scandinavian |
| nurseryman | gardener, horticulturist, florist, landscape gardener, nursery worker |
| nymphomaniac | *derogatory* |
| | |
| oarsman | rower |
| obese | use only in medical context |
| odd man | extra person; eccentric or unorthodox person |
| office boy/girl | office helper, assistant, aide, runner |
| of the feminine persuasion | female |
| of the masculine persuasion | male |
| oilman | oil driller, oil executive, oil-field worker |

| | |
|---|---|
| old fogy | old man, senior, elder |
| old lady | old woman, senior, elder |
| old maid | single woman |
| oldster | senior, elder |
| old wives' tale | superstition, folklore |
| old-womanish | *define* |
| ombudsman | researcher, mediator |
| organization man | loyal employee, team player |
| Oriental | Asian (Chinese, Japanese, Vietnamese, Cambodian, etc.) |
| outdoorsman | outdoors person, naturalist |
| out of wedlock | *eliminate* |
| over- | *avoid over-sized, over-active, over-eater, over-weight, over anything (over what?)* |
| paperboy | paper carrier, paper deliverer |
| patrolman | patrol or police officer, guard, sentry |
| patron, patroness | sponsor, backer, customer, benefactor, donor, supporter |
| patronize | protect, support, benefit, back, donate, foster, trade with; condescend to |
| paymaster | cashier, treasurer, accountant |
| P.C. | see *politically correct* |
| Peeping Tom | voyeur, snoop, eavesdropper |
| penman | writer, secretary, copyist |
| penmanship | handwriting, script, hand, calligraphy |
| physically challenged | *eliminate* |
| piece (woman) | *derogatory* |
| pig (woman) | *derogatory* |
| pinup girl | *derogatory* |
| pit man | theater prompter, stockbroker |
| pitchman | solicitor, barker, salesperson |
| plainclothesman | police officer, detective, operative, investigator, sleuth, undercover officer |
| playboy/girl | playmate, pleasure seeker, reveler, merrymaker, carouser |
| plowman/boy | plower, agriculturist, farmer, tiller |

| | |
|---|---|
| poetess | poet |
| policeman | police officer, constable (*Brit.*), detective |
| politically correct | courteous, respectful |
| political man | politician |
| poor man | beggar, street person |
| postman | postal carrier, postal clerk, mail deliverer, postal employee |
| postmaster/mistress | post office manager |
| powder puff (woman) | *derogatory* |
| prehistoric man | prehistoric people, humanlike primates, Stone (Ice, Bronze, Iron) Age people; the Neanderthals, the Cro-magnons, etc. |
| pressman | press operator, printer; newspaper person |
| priestess | priest |
| prioress | prior |
| prodigal son | prodigal child (except in biblical reference) |
| proprietress | proprietor |
| prostitute | working woman, sex worker, hired woman |
| publicity man | publicist |
| pussy (woman) | *derogatory* |
| quail (woman) | *derogatory* |
| queen (male) | cross dresser, transvestite |
| queen bee (woman) | *derogatory* |
| queenly | dignified, regal, noble |
| queen's English | proper English |
| queer | homosexual |
| radarman | radar operator, radar technician, air-traffic controller |
| radioman | radio operator, disk jockey, announcer |
| railroad man | railroad worker, railroader, engineer |
| ranchman | farmer, cattle raiser, rancher, ranch hand |
| rangerman | range rider, ranger, range hand |
| re-man (v.) | re-staff |

| | |
|---|---|
| Red Man | Native American, American Indian |
| Redskin | *eliminate as American Indian and as sports title* |
| renaissance man | renaissance person, individual with wide knowledge and skills |
| repairman | repairer, fixer, technician |
| restaurant man | restaurant owner/worker, restaurateur |
| retarded | use only in medical context |
| rewrite man | rewriter, reviser, editor |
| rib (wife) | *derogatory* |
| rifleman | shooter, soldier |
| right-hand man | assistant, key person, right arm |
| rocket man | rocketeer, astronaut, cosmonaut |
| saleslady/man | clerk, sales agent, representative |
| satyr (man) | *derogatory* |
| satyriasis | *derogatory* |
| scarlet woman | *derogatory* |
| schoolboy/girl | student, school child |
| schoolman | academic, scholar, teacher, professor |
| schoolmarm | school teacher |
| Scotchman | Scots person, Scot |
| scullery maid | scullery worker |
| sculptress | sculptor |
| seaman | sailor, mariner |
| seamanship | sailing ability, marine expertise |
| seamstress | sewer, mender, garmentmaker |
| seductress | seducer |
| seigneur | person of rank, landowner |
| seigniorage | rights of landowners |
| selectman | representative, board officer |
| self-made man | self-made person, entrepreneur |
| serviceman | service member, member of the military (soldier, sailor, marine, air force); servicer, repairer, service/repair person; plumber, carpenter, electrician, etc. |
| sex kitten | *derogatory* |
| sheepman | shepherd, sheep herder, sheep raiser, sheep rancher |

| | |
|---|---|
| she/he, her/him | see Appendix |
| shepherdess | shepherd |
| shipmaster | commander, captain |
| shoeshine boy | shoeshiner, bootblack |
| shopgirl | shopkeeper, clerk |
| short | *(compared to what?)* |
| showman | actor, performer; director; producer |
| showmanship | showiness, talent, dramatics, stage presence |
| shrew (woman) | *derogatory* |
| siren (woman) | *derogatory* |
| sissy | gentle, feminine child |
| sisterly | define |
| sister plant | nuclear power plant |
| sister ship | co-ship |
| skipper's daughters (*Naut.*) | whitecaps, rough sea |
| skirt (woman) | *derogatory* |
| skirt chaser | *derogatory* |
| sleeping beauty | sleeper, sleepyhead |
| slut | *derogatory* |
| snowman | snow creation, snowperson, snow figure |
| social man | social person, mixer |
| softer sex | *derogatory* |
| son-of-a-bitch | *derogatory* |
| son-of-a-gun | *derogatory* |
| son of the soil | farmer, peasant |
| song-and-dance man | singer and dancer |
| songstress | singer |
| sons of God, sons of Martha, sons of Norway, sons of the devil, etc. | children of… |
| sorceress | sorcerer |
| sound man | sound technician |
| spaceman | astronaut, cosmonaut |
| spinster | single or unmarried woman |
| spinsterhood | state of being single |
| spoiled (child) | troubled, angry, favored |
| spokesman | spokesperson, speaker, representative |
| sportsman | outdoors person, sports person; |

| | |
|---|---|
| | hunter, fisher, etc. |
| sportsmanship | fair play |
| squaw (woman) | *derogatory* |
| squeeze (woman) | *derogatory* |
| stableboy/man | stable tender, stable cleaner |
| stag (man) | *derogatory* |
| stallion (man) | *derogatory* |
| starlet | young star, young actor |
| statesman | leader, diplomat, public figure, politician |
| statesmanship | statecraft, diplomacy, leadership |
| stationmaster | dispatcher, station operator, station official |
| steersman | steerer, pilot, operator |
| stewardess | steward, flight attendant |
| stockman | stock raiser, stockkeeper; inventory person |
| Stone Age Man | Stone Age beings, primitives |
| straight man | stooge, set-up, shill |
| straw man | weak adversary |
| streetwalker | sex worker |
| striptease | stripper |
| strongman | giant, strong person, bully |
| stud (man) | *derogatory* |
| stud muffin | *derogatory* |
| stuntgirl/man | stunt performer |
| suffragette | suffragist |
| suffragettism | suffrage |
| sugar (woman) | *derogatory* |
| sugar daddy | *derogatory* |
| suitor (man) | *derogatory* |
| superioress | superior |
| superman/woman | superior being |
| sweetie (woman) | *eliminate, except as genderless intimate term* |
| switchman | switcher, railroad worker |
| swordsman | swordholder, combatant, fencer |
| tallyman/woman | tallyer |
| T and A (woman) | *derogatory* |
| tart (woman) | *derogatory* |
| taskmaster | overseer, tyrant, boss |

| | |
|---|---|
| taxman | tax agent, tax preparer, tax consultant |
| teenybopper | young person, teenager, young man or woman |
| telephone man | telephone installer, telephone repairer, telephone servicer |
| temptress | tempter |
| testatrix (*Law*) | testator |
| theaterman | theater operator, manager, director, producer |
| the wife | wife |
| tigress | tiger |
| timberman | timber worker, forester, woodcutter |
| to a man | to a person |
| toastmaster/mistress | head speaker, toast maker, coordinator, announcer, emcee |
| Toastmaster/Toastmistress | (legal names of organizations) |
| tomato (woman) | *derogatory* |
| tomboy | active child |
| Tom, Dick and Harry | everyone, ordinary people, people in general |
| tootsie | *derogatory* |
| townsman | townsperson, citizen |
| tradeswoman/man | tradesperson, trader, vendor, merchant |
| trainman, trainmaster | conductor, switcher, dispatcher, engineer |
| tramp (woman) | *derogatory* |
| traveling man | traveling person, traveler, salesperson, sales rep |
| trencherman | hearty eater |
| tribesman | member of a tribe |
| trick | man who buys sex |
| trigger man | assassin, hoodlum |
| trollop | *derogatory* |
| turfman | jockey, rider, horse racer |
| two-man, three-man | two-seated, two-person, three-person, etc. |
| Uncle Sam | U.S. or United States government |
| Uncle Tom | *derogatory* |

| | |
|---|---|
| underclassman | undergraduate, member of the lower levels |
| undercover man | undercover agent, officer |
| unfeminine | *define* |
| union man | union member, union worker, card holder |
| unladylike | *define* |
| unmanly | *define* |
| unwed mother | mother |
| upperclassman | member of the junior or senior (upper) class, older student |
| usherette | usher |
| utility man | general utility, utility person |
| vamp (woman) | *derogatory* |
| vestal virgin | *derogatory* |
| victress | victor |
| villainess | villain |
| virgin (woman) | *derogatory* |
| virginal, virginhood | *eliminate in reference to women* |
| vixen (woman) | *derogatory* |
| waitress | waiter, wait person, server, service person |
| wallflower (woman) | *derogatory* |
| war horse (woman) | *derogatory* |
| war paint (cosmetics) | *derogatory* |
| washerwoman | washer, launderer |
| watchman | guard, watchkeeper |
| water boy | water carrier |
| waterman | boater, rower |
| weak sister | weakling, coward |
| weaker sex | *derogatory* |
| wear the pants | dominate, take the lead |
| weatherman/girl | weathercaster, forecaster, meteorologist, weather reporter |
| well done, for a woman | well done! |
| Welshman | Welsh person |
| wench (woman) | *derogatory* |
| wenching | *derogatory* |
| wheelsman | steerer, pilot |
| whipping boy | scapegoat |

| | |
|---|---|
| white man | Caucasian, light-skinned person |
| whop (Italian) | *derogatory* |
| whore | *derogatory* (use sex worker) |
| widower, widowman | widow |
| wifely | *explain* |
| wild man | wild person |
| wingman | pilot, flier, aviator |
| wise guy | wisecracker, jokester |
| wise man | sage, wise person, learned one |
| witch (woman) | *derogatory* |
| wolf (man) | *derogatory* |
| woman architect/painter/ driver/boater, etc. | architect, painter, driver, boater, etc. |
| woman of the street | sex worker |
| woman's auxiliary | auxiliary |
| woman's place | *designate* |
| woman's work | work |
| womanish, womanly | *define, explain* |
| woodsman | forester, timber worker, outdoors person, hunter |
| working mother | worker, employed person, laborer |
| working man | worker, employed person, laborer |
| workman | worker, laborer, attendant, deliverer, line worker, production worker, etc. |
| workmanlike | skillful |
| workmanship | expertise, skill |
| workmen's compensation | workers' compensation |
| yachtsman | yachter, boater, captain, skipper |
| yardman | yard worker, landscaper |
| yardmaster | yard operator, manager |
| yeoman | attendant, assistant, clerk, farmer, guard |
| yes man | endorser, supporter, follower |
| yokefellow | companion, co-worker |

# Words to use with care and accuracy:

—*Religions groups*

Baptist ... Buddhist ...Catholic... Christian ... Episcopalian ... religious fanatic ... Gentile ... Hindu ... Jew ... Methodist ...Muslim... pagan ... Presbyterian ...

—*Physicality*

disabled ... blind ... crippled...deaf ... dwarf ... little people ... midget

—*People's size*

bulky ... fat ... giant ... hefty ... large size ... lanky ... over-eater ... over-sized ... short ... shrimp ... skinny ... woman's size, or other words referring to body shape

—*Sexual orientation*

gay ... homosexual ... lesbian ... queer ... transvestite or other words referring to sexual identity

—Aging people

Elder ... senior ... crone ... solon ... fogy

**Also be careful how you use these words as quick labels:**

—*dark skinned person* — African-American, Afro-American, Jamaican, Caribbean, colored (which color?)

—*light skinned person* — Euro-American ... Canadian ... Scandinavian ... white (how white?)

—*European* — Italian ... French ... German ... Scandinavian / Norwegian / Swede / Dane / Finn

—*Oriental* — Asian ... Pacific Rim ... Japanese ... Chinese ... Vietnamese ... Cambodian ... Filipino or Phillipino ... Korean ... Pacific Islander (does that include Hawaiian?)

—*Hispanic* — Latino ... Chicano ... Mexican ... South American ... Spaniard ... Portuguese

—*Middle-Easterner* — Arab ... Israeli ... Palestinian ... Greek ... Albanian ... Saudi ... Iraqi ... East Indian ... Pakistani ...

—*American* — Southerner ... Easterner ... Westerner ... Northerner ... Canadian ... South American ... Argentinian ... Brazilian ... Guatemalan ... Honduran ... (or does Central America belong above with Hispanic?)

Did you realize how many labels are used in everyday conversation? Remember: labels don't provide all the information.

# Index

189